ROOTED AGAINST THE

Beacon Press · Boston

Gloria Wade-Gayles

Wind

PERSONAL ESSAYS

Beacon Press
25 Beacon Street
Boston, Massachusetts 02108-2892

Beacon Press books
are published under the auspices of
the Unitarian Universalist Association of Congregations.

01 00 99 98 97 96   8 7 6 5 4 3 2 1

Text design by Christopher Kuntze
Composition by Wilsted & Taylor

Library of Congress Cataloging-in-Publication Data
can be found on page 198.

For my students

Contents

To the Reader

I am looking at the typed manuscript, which is now the book you are holding in your hands, and wondering whatever possessed me to share in so personal a way with people I do not know and will never meet. "Possessed" is an appropriate word because as I wrote, I had the strangest feeling that I was dancing in an African ritual that wards off evil spirits. I removed my clothes, making myself naked, because that is what the priestesses who were in charge of the drums said I must do if I wanted to be safe, healed, whole, and clear in vision when the ritual ends. There is power in the ritual, they explained, striking the drums with loving hands, only when it is witnessed by the village, for who we are and who we want to become must be located where the people are.

You are my village. You witnessed the ritual, but I believe you also participated in it, for in these difficult times, four years before the twenty-first century, who in the village does not need to be safe, healed, whole, and clear in vision. I speak out of a sense of connection with you when I say that I believe many of my experiences and concerns are yours as well. Perhaps, like me, you want to gather with the people and chant to the rhythms of drums that understand: "So much there is I want to say, and must say." Perhaps, like me, you want to know not only how to dance in the new century, but also what you can do to ensure that the rhythms will be ones to which the people can dance standing on their feet and moving bodies that are whole, not broken. Perhaps, like me, you have come to accept that we can never dress ourselves in any clothes until/unless we become naked. I did that in this ritual in order to put on the right clothes for these un-right times, knowing, as the drums told me, that right clothes are made only when the past and the present work together with threads of love for the people. In this ritual, I am trying to earn the right to wear those clothes.

When I look at the manuscript that way, which is the only way the "possession" makes possible, I dance naked without apology, without regret or shame, and with passion.

1

Who Says
an Older Woman
Can't/Shouldn't
Dance?

When you are fifty and over, people seem to feel the need to tell you how well you are physically wearing/weathering your age. Their evaluations are compliments, or perhaps I should say "condiments"—thick catsup, sweet jellies, creamy sauces, and brown gravy needed for meals we did not order and do not relish. In other words, they are intended to make palatable the unappetizing reality of growing older. "Don't let this go to your head," they caution, "but you really look good for your age." The compliments, so unoriginal, so tired, so cliché-ish, so focused exclusively on the physical, are, I suppose, the answers women want to hear when they ask, "Mirror, mirror on the wall, who's the best preserved of them all?" Those who hold the mirror for me have no idea that I am turning away in irritation. I mean, who gave them the right to assume that I need to be reassured about the good fight I am waging against the scarring hand of time? They compliment, and I talk back to them with my inside voice:

"How do you do *it? You just don't look your age."*
[Do what? Look how?]

"You're so playful so . . . so much fun. You don't act your age."
[I came out of my mother's womb playful, and pray tell
me why I can't remain so at my age, and says who?]

"No gray hair? Come on now. I know you are using a rinse."
[Are you asking me or telling me?]

*"It's the natural! That's the magic. People do say a natural
takes years off a black woman's face. When I see how young
it makes you look, I seriously consider giving up my perm."*
[Give up your perm! You wouldn't go natural if
guidelines for the crowning of Miss America required
that the tiara be placed only on top of peppercorn.]

*"You're the kind of older woman who could drive a young
man crazy."*
[That's supposed to be a compliment? All he needs to
be is *young*, but I have to be some kind of special-old!
Exactly what bait am I using to get this so-called catch?]

"It's amazing. You still look sexy."
[You need a crash course in sexuality after fifty.]

*"Me. Personally, I prefer older women, unless they're fat.
Now that, even in a young woman, turns me off."*
[When was the last time you stepped on the scale,
I wonder.]

*"Girl, you're lucky. You don't have to worry about lying
on top."*
[Lying on top? What in the world is *that* about?]
"You know. When we lean over, our sag really sags."

When a woman reaches fifty, her age becomes "the talk of the
town," and most of the people doing the talking are other
women, not men. To be sure, men are curious about our age,
but they express their curiosity in ways allowed only to their
gender. Some of them are bold enough to ask directly, "How
old are you?" We need not answer, for as the eyes undress us
they say, "You couldn't be more than . . . but it really won't
matter when the lights are out." In other words, men flirt.
Women, however, pry, and understandably so because we
know that asking a woman her age can be as invasive as
a gynecological exam. Consequently, we are forced, as men
are not, to use search-and-find techniques which would be
offensive if they weren't so transparent and silly.

*We measure the number and length of wrinkles on a
woman's face as if, like rings around a tree, they indicate
the exact number of years lived. Laughter, however, throws
off our computation, turning parallels into a thicket of lines
we can neither count nor measure.*

*We conduct clandestine research on her life which aids us
with our math. "Let's see now. Her children are _____
and that would make her at least _____, and since she
graduated college in _____, . . ." Or, "She was in the
class with _____, maybe a year ahead or behind, but*

definitely around the same time, and since _____
is _____, *she would have to be at least* _____."

*We disclose in order to get a disclosure. For example, we
share our disappointment in having been "done in" on our
driver's license. Showing the unbecoming mug shot, but
really the year beneath it, we ask, "Did they do you in, too?"
I don't play show-'n-tell: "Worse, girl. Mine is so bad I
won't let anyone see it, not even traffic cops."*

Am I running from my age?

Can we accept our age and at the same time reject assumptions about age? Really, what is a woman over fifty supposed to do? Go silent? 'Fess up? Cop an attitude? Be coquettish? Or lie? As in—shave a year or two? "Yes, lie," I think to myself, because even if we tell the truth, the assumption is that we always lie. That is what we hear in recycled material for sexist jokes about older women and in beauty myth commercials. The former fills clubs with loud laughter; the latter fills already fat pockets with profit. Since I stopped going to clubs (it's an age thing, you see), I don't know the latest old woman joke, but beauty myth commercials? That's a different story altogether. I can close my eyes and see a flawless face attached to flowing hair (fragmented woman) whispering seductively, "Don't lie about your age, defy it." In all things, women are expected to be pure like driven snow—gotta find another image!—but when it comes to age, we are allowed the transgression of a lie. This being the case, if/when we lie, we can say, in truth, "The culture made me do it."

Am I running from my age?

This culture-induced shaving goes well with the American sport of guessing a woman's age, and the playing field is wherever we find ourselves. I find that the sport brings out the mischief in me. When my friends play backcourt, aiming for my birth year, I play net, foiling their attempts to know. That is what I did in Mississippi (state changed to protect the not-innocent) when a friend attempted to *see* the age on my driver's license. I was on tour at the time and splurging a bit in a department store which was offering end-of-the-season sales prices that made Filene's Basement seem like Saks or Nieman Marcus. I mean, these were *incredible* bargains. With my friend's assistance (because I am color blind and style ignorant), I selected several outfits, the total price of which exceeded the amount of cash I could spend on something not included in my budget. Having decided that plastic is the root of all evil, I reached into my purse for my checkbook.

"Do you take out-of-town checks?" I asked the saleslady, looking with envy at her manicured nails and rethinking (but only for a second) my decision not to wear acrylic.

From rote memory, she recited responses learned in training. "We take Visa, MasterCard, Discover, American Express . . ."

"Not credit cards," I said. "Checks. Do you take out-of-town checks?"

"Sure," she said. "All you need is a driver's license and a major credit card."

A driver's license? Eureka! My absolute age was within reach of my friend's eyes. I could feel her breathing hard, almost salivating over the find, when I laid the license on the counter, face up, teasing her. At the very second her contorted neck goosed its way over the plastic square, her breathing increasing in tempo, I mischievously turned my birth year face down in the cashier's hand. And why not? My age did not reduce the price of the clothes or improve the quality of our friendship.

Each time I hear "you look good," I hear the loud follow-up silence that is actually a blank I have to fill in with my age, which, in my over-fifty way of thinking, proves that my friends are sleuthing rather than complimenting. And since they are so very serious about their work, "over fifty" cannot fill in the blank. That's only a clue, not the real find. They want to know how *much* over fifty, down to the month, the week, the day, the minute, the second, perhaps, that I came out of my mother's womb and screamed that I was a live birth. Sometimes I think true-false would be more creative than fill-in-the-blank, or, if not more creative, certainly easier for those of us who do not feel compelled to say or write our exact age. Just think about it. "You are fifty-five. True or false?" All we need do is circle a word. We can tell the truth without disclosing our exact age.

Am I running from my age?

"Girl, if I looked as good as you, I would tell the whole world how old I am," a friend says. I want to tell her (perhaps I did) that "good" strains at being a compliment. I learned this four years ago in a chance meeting with an old friend (old as in, I had known him for many years, rather than his life totaled many years) in a bank parking lot on a sunny July afternoon. I had not seen him for at least five years and there he was, directly in front of me, rushing to the bank, at 3:55, to get inside before the guard locked out late-comers like us. When last I saw him, he was a smooth voice emanating from the pulpit of a black Baptist church and a warm smile signaling me out of a group of visitors for a special embrace. What delight to see him indistinguishable among laypeople, without his black robe and his word of God. I rushed toward him and gave him an embrace I know now was much too tight. "Bill, you look *so* good!" I said. He returned the embrace and then directed me, politely, to the back door through which my compliment had entered: "*Good*, Gloria, is what we say to people who are growing old."

Good. Yes, that's an age-word! How surprised (and delighted?) I am that my children never say, "Mom, you look good." Instead, they say, "Mom, you look great," never adding "for your age." They can fill in the blank, for my birth year is face up in their hands, but without any coaching from me, they protect it as much as I do. There must be something in my demeanor that prevents them from using any form of the word "old," which is a radical departure from their obsession with the word during their preteen years. Then "old" was the word they seemed to have coined all by themselves, with the help of their peers, to stake out a claim for some kind of autonomy in a world peopled with "adults" who were agents of interference they could not shake. Then "old" seemed to connote authority more than calendar years, unless it was preceded by "real," which was used to describe adults who, as venerable elders, could do whatever they wished almost with impunity. Now in their early twenties, my children describe *things* rather than *people* as "old," giving the word new definitions: frayed, too small, outdated, or in serious need of repair, as in "old" sweater, "old" coat, "old" typewriter, or the "old" car I drive.

I have no doubt they used "pretty" when I and they were younger, an expression of their love for me rather than a statement of fact about my appearance. They internalized the be-pretty requirement for mothers. "Pretty" mothers, our children learn in this culture, can greatly improve their social status. "Your mama is pretty!" means she's the one peers choose as chauffeur for a field trip, giving them a sense of importance they might not otherwise have; and "I bet you're gonna look like your mother when you get old" polishes the mirror in which they see themselves. While having a pretty mother (pretty here for black women meaning not overweight, not too dark, attractively coiffeured, well-dressed, and young-looking) might not protect them from Mama-insulting jokes (that is, the "dozens"), it might dull or shorten the cutting knife. There are no dozens for fathers. There is no be-pretty requirement for men.

I didn't attempt to meet the be-pretty requirement—perhaps because I thought I couldn't but mainly because I didn't think it gave my statement on self the right punctuation. For whatever the reason, I chose, as my mother did (But *she* was pretty!) to be a plain woman. I wore very little makeup, did not perm my hair, and had a blind spot when it came to fashion. Among a community of mothers, I probably stood out as a "hippie." I know it is foolish of me now to wonder how I looked then, but "rewinds," I have come to realize, go with the territory of fifty. Reclaim, recapture, recollect, remember, we are taught, because fifty begins the quick slide into forgetfulness. I rewind to my thirties and, yes, there I am, an unforgivably plain woman.

Choosing to be plain when I was younger was an act of defiance with few if any consequences, but choosing to be plain now that I am older could be much too risky. After all, makeup, hairstyles, and dress can do wonders for an older woman. Is that what my neighbor in Talladega, Alabama, was trying to tell me when she advised me to wear makeup, even arch my eyebrows? A woman past thirty who refuses to beautify herself, she said, is either crazy or incredibly vain. Years later, I tried to follow her advice, only to learn that not every woman looks good arched.

I expected a gloriously improved Gloria after my dear friend, Ann-Rebecca, the children's godmother, made me over when I was in my late thirties. She worked lovingly (more important, carefully) with the sharp razor blade, removing thick brows and, with perfection, arching the remaining hair. She worked in front of the mirror in the master bathroom while the children sat in front of the television in the den. "Are you ready yet, Mommie?" Monica asked more than once. Finally, I had a new face! "Come see how pretty Mommie looks," I called to them. I will never forget the look of fear on my daughter's face or the tears. "Mommie, you look like a witch." That was the last time I went down that avenue of beauty. I entered fifty bushy-eyed, and plain.

"Did you ever have to defend me?" I want to ask my children now that I am older. "Did anybody ever play the dozens on you? Back when I was young, did you ever wish I looked different? Did you . . . ?" But why ask when their eyes say, "You look great, Mom," but "No more years, please." It is that look all of us have when we see our parents becoming older. It is concern. It is fear. Addition of years eventually brings us frighteningly close to our mortality.

How fast the years went. Only yesterday, it seems, I was the young mother whose two-piece bathing suit my children held onto in swimming lessons at the neighborhood YMCA, or whose legs in short shorts they saw racing toward them when they crossed the finish line in a high school track meet. Only yesterday, I was skipping rope with them, banging backboards, climbing over rocks in a tame Georgia pond, beating them to the door on a summer's day, and cheering with them at their high school football games. Of course, they don't do those things themselves any longer. They, too, are older, but they are older-young. According to our reading of age in America, I am older on my way to being old.

The big *Five O* is the culprit. It doesn't matter that the graying of America has changed the line of demarcation between still-capable and over-the-hill, making fifty a young age as it was not in the past. I mean, is fifty still the stopping age for being alive and active and not-yet old? Nor does it matter that women have challenged the nonsense by claiming and celebrating their arrival at fifty. Our culture is so stuck in patriarchal mire about so many things, most especially age, that the big *Five O* remains the culprit, and when we reach it, according to the assumption, the decline begins. That is what we are taught in America. At *fifty*, the decline begins.

Maturity, *the magazine published by the Association of Retired Persons, features the faces and brief bios of women and men who have reached "the big Five O!" Not Five* O, *but Five "Oh" as in, it seems, "Oh no!"*

"Many people fifty and over,*" Ed McMahon says, the premiums moving on the screen beneath the policy he holds, "don't think they can qualify for health insurance without having to answer embarrassing questions about . . . ," but there is hope in a policy that will bleed our blood. At* fifty *we are a risk even for those who never take risks with money.*

A national leader reaches her fiftieth birthday and it becomes national news. People respond: "I didn't know she was that old." Or, a friend discloses that she is forty-five and people respond, "I didn't know she was that close to fifty."

Articles entitled "Women Who Are Young After Fifty" *flood magazines, some of which are* not *tabloids.*

Books on how to enjoy sex after fifty *constitute a large market in our nation (though many of the readers stealing a look in mall bookstores are in their teens).*

Outfits for the "mature woman" are outfits for women who are at least fifty. *Mature is not attractive.*

In our obsession with age, fifty—*half a century!*—means that as we add years, we subtract capabilities. Fifty-something (even if it is fifty-plus-one) means being close to sixty, which begins the terrifying move to seventy, which traumatizes many of us because everyone knows—since the Bible told us so—that God promised us only seventy-plus years on this earth. Even forty-something now frightens us, and thirty-something is not far behind. How young they are, and yet my children and their friends and my former students lament in their early and mid twenties, "I'm almost thirty!" To be "thirty-something," we learned from the popular television show by that name, is to be close to the problem arena of middle age. And now there is "Twenty-Something." Age is a national obsession.

Correction: *Aging*. That is the politically correct word for the addition of years to our lives, but I find it a sterile word, and therefore appropriate, I suppose, for the kind of reality women are supposed to have as we become older. It is flat like our breasts which (without implants) sag, cold like our feet, which we must cover with socks or risk "turning off" the man with whom we sleep, and colorless like the lives we are supposed to live. It lacks poetry, color, and movement. It is a neutering word that places us in clinical categories: premenopausal, menopausal, postmenopausal, losing this and needing that. Like a cold stethoscope pressed against our bosom, *"aging"* listens for a weaker heartbeat; or like an unfeeling gloved hand, it enters those parts of ourselves where we are most vulnerable. How much like "ailing" it sounds. Was *aging* always the naming word?, I wonder. What was the word for my mother's generation and her mother's? Has anyone conducted research on the different words for this "affliction" and examined them in a political context? Always, there is a political context.

What about "senior citizen"? Well, it *is* a kinder term, but, unfortunately, it does not always mean "senior" in ability or position. It directs our attention to retirement and to residence in senior citizen high-rises, and, in the minds of many people, that means diminution of capabilities.

"It's a shame," my mother said, "the way we retire people before we should." We give legal clout to the myth that "mind damage" comes by an age arbitrarily determined and applied to everyone. Without a paper trail on poor performance, we put people "out to pasture" automatically at sixty-five, or seventy. My God did I wish when I was forty to have the analytic ability, the sharpness, and the retention of vital information my mother had at seventy! And how I do envy today the mind, the energy, and the clarity of friends decades older than I. How foolish we are to use calendar years as the measurement of anyone's talents, capabilities, or value in society.

Instead of saying that people are aging, or growing old, why don't we say that years have been added to their lives? Yes, why not describe/name the process as "the addition of years"? That is benign and precise. It makes a statement of fact *objectively and quantitatively* reached, predicting no absolutes as to resultant limitations and crippling restrictions of an arbitrary but definite age.

Am I running from my age?

A friend accused me of going the route of euphemism ("the addition of years") in order to avoid the path my age is furrowing for me. She had a good argument: euphemisms might keep us in denial, but they don't alter that which we deny. I understood her point and even helped her develop it. "I know that using 'resting place' rather than 'cemetery,'" I said, "does not change what we experience when we lose a loved one. Everyone knows that! And I know that no matter what we call it, we get older every single day that we breathe." But in my defense, I emphasized the importance of naming-words; they carry nuances, attitudes, assumptions, and expectations, and ultimately they shape behavior. They can liberate or imprison. The word "aging," in my opinion, imprisons.

And double standards shaped by gender throw away the key. To wit: being male in patriarchy is an advantage and being female, a disadvantage, in *everything*, even in the God-decreed process of adding years to your life.

A man in his seventies, deep wrinkles and all, can become president of the nation. If a woman could jump the gender hurdle (and that would require wings), she would see a higher hurdle of age. In other words, if a woman ever becomes president, it is doubtful that she will wear deep wrinkles.

A man in his fifties or sixties (even early seventies) sits at the anchor desk, dispensing news and analysis often "decorated" by a woman younger than he in years. A woman in her fifties who wears even faint signs of age roves from crisis to crisis, standing rather than sitting in front of the camera. (If she is slightly "overweight" and not so "pretty," she will rove even at pre-fifty; if she is all of this and black, she probably won't rove at all.)

Age-and-gender biases are invisible particles in the air we breathe; they get into our bloodstream and change the chemistry of our attitudes toward other people and, if we are women, toward ourselves. In the media, they are the stark and seductive images that turn on the projector, amplify the sound, color the scenes, and write scripts that give leading lines to women who are young and only a nod to women who are older. To men, however, they give the enviable ability to be more attractive, more sexy, more suave, more everything desired precisely because they are older, even if age walks in deep crevices on their face. Like aged wine, older men, mellowed and smooth, become a desired vintage. Older women, on the other hand, are the tasteless wine, rendered flat from having been open so many years. Proof is the saying that older men are sexy, so much so that young women sometimes choose older men—graying temples and all—for their sex fantasies. There is no such saying for older women, and if they, by chance, enter the fantasies of younger men, we charge, "Oedipal!"

A dramatic example of media rendering of age and sexuality is the recent box-office hit *The Bridges of Madison County*, which received, and deserved, accolades for its departure from media commodification of lovemaking as hard sex that bones, bangs, and knocks, and therefore sells. It contains no rough gymnastics, no full nudity, no hint of dominance, no on-top/on-bottom positioning, only sweet ecstasy. The lovers are one body oiled satin by hypnotic and seductive intimacy. They perform the love dance, vertically and horizontally, slowly and gently, with pleasure giving pleasure. And when the dance ends, satisfied, they love again, this time with light strokes and color-painting words.

But the film stops short of challenging gender assumptions about age which patriarchy creates and perpetuates. Both characters are middle-aged, but only Clint Eastwood is visibly so. His wrinkles are deep, promising passion. Meryl Streep's wrinkles, by contrast, are faint, lying like pencil marks on her epidermis. Only a hair ribbon is missing from the image of a middle-aged woman looking younger than her years. Visible age on women is a sexual turn-off rather than a sexual turn-on.

Racism ensures that there be no Eastwood versions of sexual passion colored black. Black men as gentle lovers capable of magical intimacy rarely, if ever, appear on the silver screen, and our affected minds lead many of us to doubt that they appear in our bedrooms. It is all bump-and-grind with/for us, rumor has it, and songs sing it, even popular songs written and performed by us. "Ain't nothing wrong with a little bump and grind" and "Pump it up" are two mild examples of this vinegar taste of hard black sex packaged for a good sell.

Nor are there Streep versions of older black women. Down through the centuries, we have been the "darker berry" (an *object*!) that gives "sweeter" juice, and recently we have become "freaks, superfreaks" no man would dare "take home to Mama." The "berry" and the "freak," like the pumping-grinding brother, are young. When we become older, we are neither berries nor freaks. We are, instead, neutered uncles and mammies. Bandannas, not ribbons, and aprons of asexuality, not dresses that catch the wind, are our media costumes. And how appropriate this is for a nation that created the asexual mammy in order to conceal the very sexual requirements of her role in the big house.

To be black, woman, and older is to be plunged whole into toxic waters from head to torso to heel, and we must find creative ways to prevent the damage from being consummate, for this triple jeopardy removes us from what this culture values: being white, being male, and being young. This is the case in the white world outside our communities, and no less so within our communities, for we have yet to develop immunities to the ailments white America suffers. We love young as much as we love white and we continue to privilege male over female.

Of course, we put the problem squarely on the shoulders of "the man." Before we were assimilated into white America, we say, or before we were Europeanized, we say, we valued the wisdom and beauty of older women. Like syphilis, we say, obsession with age is a disease we contracted from "them." My over-fifty way of thinking tells me that knowing who gave us the disease (as if we actually contracted it from "them" in particular rather than from human beings in general) does not remove it from our bloodstream. Once we have it, the search for a cure cannot take us away from ourselves. And a cure we *do* need. Older black women are the butt of offensive jokes in the black community. "Ain't nothing an *old* black woman can do for me" is a common punch line in comic routines, as is "Ain't nothing a *real* black woman can do for me" ("real" meaning "very" or "too").

Moms Mabley turned the age punch line on its head.

Donning dress and mannerisms that accentuated assumed limitations of her race and her age, and using a mop and bucket as props, she pulled audiences from their seats with her gummed recitation of the uselessness of old men. Maybe they could bring her a cup of coffee, but even that was questionable. What "Moms wants, children" is a "*young* man." But that is not what a black "Moms" will get. The truth is, black men as a group are less likely than white men as a group to become involved with older women (publicly, that is). Denied manhood in white America, they, more than white men, need a young woman to give proof of their undiminished sexuality. I do not mean to indict all black men or even most of them, as my wording "as a group" indicates, but I believe we are in denial if we do not admit the difficulty black men as a group have marrying dark, marrying "not pretty," and marrying not young.

Women, too, breathe in the toxicity. Let's face it, we have internalized double standards about age. Albeit with some difficulty, we are more likely to accept an older man (though not too old) for our daughters than an older woman for our sons. And while we don't think twice about a male friend who has taken up with a younger woman, we look with disfavor at a woman friend who is involved with a younger man.

A FRIEND: "Did you hear about _____? She's living with a man ten years her junior."

ME: "Really?" Wondering why the issue is his age rather than their cohabitation, or any other issue at all.

THE FRIEND: "I guess that's a sign of the times. There aren't many available men and . . . (a pause) we are once again imitating white women."

ME: "Frankly, I prefer older men. Actually get excited over graying temples and a smile topped by bald. But I think women should be free to do their own thing. With whomever."

I think becoming fifty made a "new woman" out of me. Shock treatment. That's what it was. I saw "Five O," I heard "half a century," and I became determined to fight the demons that frighten us about age. My retina worked better than it ever had and my ear canal became long enough to be written up in the *Guinness Book of Records*. I began to see and to hear age biases I missed in my younger years. Sometimes I wish I didn't have this worrisome thing called awareness because it critiques the very pleasure out of a movie and jangles the chord of a song. It was that way with my awareness of misogyny ("Can't you just see the movie," my children used to ask, "and forget what's gender-wrong with it?"); and it has always been that way with my awareness of racism ("Don't you think you are being racially hypersensitive?" white friends ask). Sometimes when I am weary of the weight of awareness, I tell myself, "Just forget the lyrics, girl, and go on and dance to the beat." That is what I said when I recently bought a discounted CD containing the best hits by Ray Charles. I danced, as I had many years ago, to "Smack Dab in the Middle," a favorite of mine because it is Charles at his gospel-funk best, accompanied by his talking piano rather than symphonic strings which can't talk the way only Charles can. I danced, trying to ignore that the song objectifies women, putting us in a list of things Charles desires. I danced, trying to ignore a message I was hearing for the first time: that the women are desired only if they are young. Charles sings that he wants:

> *Ten Cadillacs.*
> *A diamond mill.*
> *Ten suits of clothes*
> *To dress to kill.*
> *A ten-room house.*
> *Some barbecue.*
> *And twenty chicks*
> *Not over twenty-two.*

Am I jealous that I am not in the middle with the Cadillacs, the suits of clothes, the house, and barbecue? Naw! I don't take well to being an object. Would I like to be twenty-two again? Now *that* is a different question. I am not one of those women over fifty who have been known to say, "You couldn't pay me to be in my twenties again, what with drugs, violence, AIDS, the shortage of men! I feel sorry for this generation." They might "feel sorry for this generation," but I think they lie when they say they wouldn't like to be younger. No one welcomes the addition of years to their life. I think they lie because being in our twenties is a far greater distance from retirement, nursing homes, and the cessation of life than being in our fifties. I think they lie because being in our twenties means our parents are actively involved in our lives and we in their lives; there are no all-night prayers for their recovery from illness attributed to age. I know they lie because the loss of a parent is a trauma none of us wants to experience and from which none of us ever fully recovers. Preferring to be fifty rather than twenty-two flies in the face of logic.

I would prefer to be younger. Correction and confession: I wish I were younger and sometimes the wish brings on sadness. But on my fiftieth birthday, I accepted that numbers don't lie. "And now, Gloria," I told myself, "you are what is called an older woman." But I did not feel that the addition of years to my life had resulted in a subtraction of joys, goals, or even energy. In fact, I felt young, even more exuberant than I had been in years, and alive with passion for projects that only recently I have claimed as my own. I had reached fifty, and yet I still played tennis. I still ran up and down my steps. I still danced to fast rhythms. And I knew I was capable of marching again, facing billy clubs again, and singing from jail cells again in a new movement I believe we so desperately need. I know that I can because I am the racial kin of Septima Clark, Ella Jo Baker, and, before them and others like them, Harriet and Sojourner and the thousands unnamed. They were not twentyish when they were on the battlefield. My age, then, was a year on my driver's license, not an albatross around my neck.

That did not mean, however, that I wanted anyone to give me a party. I had the breath to extinguish fifty candles, but not the desire. Gratitude, not happiness, was the emotion I experienced. I remembered better women than I—high school and college classmates, neighbors, and friends—who did not live to be fifty, forty, and, in several cases, thirty. To lament reaching fifty would have been the ultimate in vanity and ingratitude.

When gratitude quieted my sadness, a different emotion came into play. Fear. I actually began to worry about dying. This is an understandable response, I think, given the plethora of after-fifty problems for women that saturate the media. *After fifty*, a woman must go for mammograms more frequently, and mammograms, some people believe, increase the risk of breast cancer. *After fifty*, a woman is more susceptible to heart attacks because estrogen goes, and hot flashes come with a vengeance. *After fifty*, many women must make a difficult decision: to do estrogen replacement and live with the fear of breast cancer, or not do it and live with the fear of a heart attack, as well as, though not life-threatening, the absence of pleasurable—or possible—sex. And *after fifty*, a woman must exercise her vaginal muscles in order to strengthen the bladder in order to ward off incontinence. Most advertisements for Depend feature women. Our minds can become so inundated with these reminders of how vulnerable we are to everything bad that paranoia invites them to enter our bodies which are older, but not yet afflicted.

Which is why, by fifty-two—or was it fifty-three—I became fanatical about vitamins, enzymes, and herbs that, according to books increasing daily in numbers, prevent everything from loss of memory (B-12) to high cholesterol (niacinamide), cancer (the antioxidants A, C, and E), dry skin (E), heart disease (garlic), thickened arteries (lecithin), osteoporosis (calcium plus D), or whatever (a teaspoon of apple vinegar every day). Not until I reached my mid fifties (fortunate never to have flashed hot once) did I learn to love the taste of tasteless tofu and add yams to every meal because, so say the experts, both are good estrogen-replacement foods. Where once the only magazines stuffed in my mailbox were news and scholarly ones, *Prevention* appeared, and, I confess, there were days when it assumed greater importance for me than the others. (Alas, *Prevention* has gone the way of com-modification.)

Where once I went directly to sections marked "Women's Studies," "African-American Studies," or "Classics," I entered bookstores with my eyes searching for sections containing how-to manuals, inspirational writings, and books on aging. Ask me about passages and tunnels and fountains and I can give you salient quotes from the experts.

Unfortunately, all of the experts are white women. I wonder why we are not writing books about *us* and the addition of years? As with everything else, in this, too, we are unique. We can complain that we are not in *Passages*, *The Fountain of Age*, *Salty Old Women*, and *The Beauty Myth* (which is, in its own way, about age since beauty requires youth), but we don't have a varicosed leg to stand on if we do. The way that racism exacerbates ageism, which is further exacerbated by class, is our project and nobody else's. To paraphrase Langston Hughes, somebody oughta write a book about black women coping with the addition of years, and I guess it oughta be us.

We oughta look with our own eyes at the clever ways American culture has caused all eyes to turn away from the prevention of illness and become fixed on the elimination of visible signs of aging. The inside can be collapsing, but all is well if the outside looks good. Ours is a culture of denial and fantasy, programming and profit. America sells vanity at a high cost. A billion-dollar industry (which makes the rich richer) bombards us with happy jingles, talking jars, and non-greasy liquids that, before our very eyes (on television, that is), perform miracles. They remove wrinkles, they tighten the skin, they lighten dark spots, they smooth away cellulite, they keep us dry or prevent us from becoming dry. They are miracle workers, these products, and the people who tell us so are women, pretty women, wearing just-right colors and sitting with their legs angled just right for the unseen cameras that are meant to give us these infomercials. All the women have teeth filed down and capped for the perfect smile. All the women smile, for all the women are happy that they have found the elixir of youth, and they know how to pose happy having been trained in modeling schools to do so. But they are not all the same, these women, in their skin care needs. Some have dry skin; others, oily skin; and still others, dry and oily. How amazing, they tell us, that one cream works for *all* types of skin. Most of the women are white, though occasionally one is black, but not too Africanic; or Asian, but not too Asian.

Beauty commercials get into our psyche and direct us down this aisle and up that one, delivering us to the very place where the product, expecting our arrival, jumps from the shelf into our waiting hands. Me? Spend money for a product that makes being pretty synonymous with being young, and white (or, in black magazines, white-looking), and that can't deliver on its promise of a miracle! No way! I was too self-respecting for that and, besides, I didn't need a miracle. I had no wrinkles, no graying hair, no dark age spots, no drawn neck, no dry hands, and no ravaging cellulite.

Arrogant and judgmental, I criticized women who lined their dressers with age-defying moisturizers, but when I reached my mid fifties, I had to "eat crow." Age did what age does for most of us; it crept up on me. While I was sleeping, it walked all over my face. I'd swear I went to bed one night without a wrinkle and awoke the next morning to what I thought was the imprint of the mattress on my face. Wrinkles! Not prescription creams or expensive name-brand creams, but plain ole ordinary you-buy-at-a-drugstore creams appeared on my dresser. I rationalized, there is no need to let too many wrinkles come too early if, at a small cost and without injury to my health, I can put on a little dab of cream every night and keep my face smooth. You know, it's like using Vaseline Intensive Care Lotion on my hands. I don't want dry hands; I don't want a dry face. Actually, it's a health thing, isn't it? There's nothing obsessive about that, is there? I am not trying to look young, am I?

Is that what people think, I wonder, when they see my over-fifty body wrapped in blue jeans? But I love my blue jeans, the plain ones, I mean, not the designer jeans that turn our broad hips into billboards for a white woman named Gloria or a white man named Calvin. Not the designer ones that cost a fortune. Not the designer ones that are used to sell a woman's body. Not the designer ones that are stretched tight on women's open legs (yes, ours are always open; men's are usually closed) in magazine ads. Not those jeans, but rather the ordinary, plain, and reasonably priced ones. I wear them for the same reason men have worn them for decades —they are the *only* clothing that needs limited care. You can wear a pair of blue jeans for a week (if you shower daily) and still be clean and look clean. You can dress a pair of blue jeans down or, with a colorful jacket, dress them up. You can lie on the grass in blue jeans without worrying about grass stains or work on the car without being concerned about oil stains because the amazing thing about blue jeans is that they convert a stain into a design. The more stains, the more authentic the blue jeans. I was okay with my love for blue jeans until

I heard them talk about her when she passed. "She's some fine," one of them said. "Phat," the other said. She was an older woman. In her mid fifties I would guess, her body wrapped well in a pair of blue jeans. They talked about her. "She's some fine," and then they "undressed" her. "Yeah, but wonder how she look with her pants off?" They laughed.

I felt a lump forming in my throat. Had men ever "undressed" me?, I wondered. Had they "taken off" my blue jeans and "touched" flaccid skin and sagging breasts? Did anyone, stranger or friend, think my preference for the easy-go/nonprofessional look—jeans, denim skirts, loose-fitting dresses, turtlenecks, vests with Aztec designs, blouses made for rolled-up sleeves, dangling earrings, sandals, flats—was my attempt to deny the truth about my body, my age? Should I care?

Should I care that as a black woman in her fifties, I am consigned emotionally to one of three groups? Women who are depressed, made so by loneliness, regrets, and fear of a speedy decline into emptiness. Women who are angry, made so by remembering too well who did them wrong, including themselves in the group. Women who are saintly, though I can't for the life of me understand what made this group, except perhaps the prescription that we begin preparing early for the afterlife to ensure that we walk on streets of gold rather than burn in furnaces. Saintly. Translation: bland and blind. We see no evil, speak no evil, do no evil, and for that matter, remember no past evil seen, spoken, or done. By us, that is. Saintly? Translation: asexual.

I am sometimes sad about being no longer young, but I am not depressed. Busy women usually aren't. I'm certainly not angry. Blessed women rarely are. And though I am hopelessly tied to old-fashioned notions of morality, that is, I am a "good girl," and I work hard at speaking no evil and doing no evil, I am nobody's saint. I am as human in my fifties as I was in my twenties, and, therefore, flawed.

If I am not depressed, angry, or saintly, what am I? Myself. Just an ordinary woman who, having decided not to be too concerned about this age thing, will dance to her own rhythm. Like a college administrator who was the "belle" of one of our annual Christmas parties, I am going to be myself. Regardless.

The band was playing, and we were dancing—men with women, women with women, men alone, and women alone. Just dancing. Having a ball. I sat down to get my second wind, having danced continuously to three numbers, when I heard someone at a nearby table say, "Can you believe the way she is dressed?" I looked at the center floor and saw her whirling. She was in another world. What daring, I thought to myself, noticing for the first time that she was dressed in a black microminiskirt and in black semisheer tights. "That outfit is what the students wear," I heard the critic say. I said nothing. Instead, I bounded up from my table and bopped my way to the dance floor. I made my statement in my dance. I danced wildly, knowing that people might think I was competing with her when all along I was affirming her, and myself.

Coming from a culture, or a community, or perhaps an era, that passed censure on women over fifty who acted or dressed too young for their age, I have to forgive myself at the end of each day for the way I am. I rewind the tape of my memories and hear women from my youth excoriating one among them who broke the rules about age-behavior and dress:

"Look at her wearing clothes like that. At her age. She's fifty if she's a day. I know it. And just look at her trying to catch a man. It's pitiful. Real sad. She better learn to look her age 'cause men don't want you even if you do dress young."

This is an early lesson in what a woman actually loses when she gets older—not her youth, but men, and since men are needed to validate a woman she also loses her worth.

I understand the reaction black women of my mother's generation had to dressing young. It signified dignity and a noble resignation to the unerring hand of time, but, more importantly, it offered proof that they had more character than white women. They were devoted to keeping their children looking good, not to keeping themselves looking good. They were anchored in family rather than propped up in front of a mirror. Unlike them, white women were incredibly vain, given to fighting age in various ways, the women said, layering on the foundation, wearing low-cut dresses, putting flat hips (ethnicity makes ours broad) into painted-on pants, and, if they had money, going under the knife. No, they did not want to be like vain white women.

But other rewinds suggest they would try to be like vain white women if doing so would give them what black women are programmed to believe white women receive from white men, even when they reach fifty: attention and affection.

"You know white women are something else. They put on bikinis and let all those wrinkles show. And you know, they think they are looking good. They can be old and ugly, but they strut around as if they're young and beautiful."

"That's what they're told from the time they're born. That they're beautiful. And don't let them be a blonde or a redhead! Then they're really ruined."

"But you know, the thing that gets me is the way white men treat them with wrinkles and all."

"I know what you mean."
*"Holding their hands and sitting in department stores
while they shop. It's something else."*

Silence.
Pain.

Perhaps I dance because many of our mothers could not,
or did not. Perhaps I dance because I am celebrating the liberation they did not experience, but wanted so desperately for
their daughters. Perhaps I dance because their struggles and
their sacrifices have blessed me with good-life rhythms they
never heard. Perhaps I dance as a way of screaming against the
dirges poor black women hear every day of their lives. Dirges
are for death, not life. I want to live. I want to live as fully at
fifty-plus, at sixty, and at seventy as I lived at twenty, thirty,
and forty. I want to live and therefore I must dance. I dance,
then, in spite of my age and because of my age.

I know I am no longer young because in my night dreams
and day fantasies I am holding an infant nestled against sagging breasts that give the aroma of love, not milk. That I am
ready and anxious to become a grandmother is the most joyous age-music to which I now dance.

I know I am no longer young because my day visions of
tomorrow show junior faculty with whom I work at Spelman
College directing programs, chairing departments, writing
books, winning awards, and heading institutions. Such joy
there is in witnessing their becoming! We should not put ourselves on a shelf when we reach a certain age, but we must

make way, prepare the way and clear the way, for younger women when their time arrives.

I know I am no longer young because my financial planning focuses on retirement, yes, but more on the future of my children and my grandchildren yet unborn. I want to leave them enough memories to last a lifetime and enough money to get them through difficult periods today's conservative politics suggest will surely come.

I know I am older when I stand naked before my mirror and see my brown, older woman's body with discerning/non-rejecting eyes. I see my hands. As I move fast toward sixty, they are designed with a network of tiny lines. They are my hands and with them I can hold myself and others.

I see my face. The lines around my mouth are deeper now than they were last year and the dark hollows beneath the eyes, a genetic trait, are darker. It is my face, and it wears the smile I give myself and others.

I see my neck. It asks for high-neck blouses and scarves that accentuate as they cover, but it rests on shoulders sturdy enough for my weight and the weight of others.

I am not depressed about being older, and yet sometimes it is my voice I hear when Nina Simone, in the deep dark chocolate of her alto, sings, "I live alone. . . . The walls talk back to me and they seem to say, 'Wasn't yesterday a better day?'" Sometimes yesterday haunts me. It is the train whistle I hear when a litany of regrets disturbs my sleep, or the train itself, grander, perhaps, than in reality, moving to places once filled with my breath and shaped by my desires. I want to board yesterday, so much do I miss the texture of the life I lived then, the joys that are now then-joys. I miss yesterday, sometimes with an ache that defies description. If only I could relive my life, so much I would say and not say, feel and not feel, think and not think, do and not do, accept and reject, learn and unlearn, struggle to keep and find the courage to release. I would be different, I tell myself in my revelry, and therefore I would come different to this new place.

But only on rare cloudy days does yesterday as longing enter my new space, slowing the rhythm of my dance, but not for long because I will not permit it to linger, not in that way. As knowledge and insight, however, it is always with me, an almanac for my now-life. This will bring rain, it tells me. That, sunshine. This will affirm. That, alienate. This will confuse. That, clarify. This advises pull back. That, hang on. This cautions, "Be still." That says, "Dance!"

We are always in the process of becoming, philosophers tell us, moving through one stage in preparation for the next, each stage having its own purpose, our understanding of which ends delusional longing for previous stages. As with nature, so, too, with humankind. There are seasons in our lives we cannot bypass. We enter them when we are supposed to and, once there, we do what we are supposed to do.

The first half-century of my life was the "yes" season. I could not shape my lips to answer "no" to others' needs or remember how to say "yes" to my own. I was always interruptible, always accessible and available, always willing to get out of a document that bore my name and pull up, on my own computer no less, someone else's document. I was like a plant from which one takes cuttings. A piece for this one. A piece for that one. A piece for those over there and these over here. Although there were times when I could feel the blade, I did not regret the cuttings. They strengthened my roots.

But there is a time when a plant should be left still, when the number of cuttings should be reduced, when it should be left undisturbed in the light of its own nourishing suns. Now is that time for me, and I am content in accepting that only now could the me-time have arrived. I believe I entered this season when I was supposed to. What remains is for me to do what I believe I am supposed to do: pick up the pen, or turn on the computer, and attempt to write.

When friends tell me that I should have tried to write years ago, planting seeds of regret in the earth of my feelings, I add rather than subtract, and the result is a full life of memories and experiences that form words and images I was not supposed to know, until now. Becoming older is a gift, not a curse, for it is that season when we have long and passionate conversations with the self we spoke to only briefly in our younger years. It could be argued that if gender politics changed, that is, if women in patriarchy weren't conditioned to be other-oriented, we could reach this season earlier in life. Perhaps that is true for some women, but not for me. Patriarchy did not force me to be maternal, and that is what I was, and am. Maternal. I chafe at the very idea that any-one would attribute this joy to patriarchy, to sexism, to re-strictions on my life. If all the rules had been different, I know that my longer conversations would have been with my loved ones, my students, and others. That was my choice, and that was my joy. It was not so much that I held the joy of writing in suspension as that the season for writing had not yet arrived.

"I can't talk to you now," I say in this season. "I'm writing."

"This is not a good weekend for a visit," I am able now to tell friends. "I am driving up to the mountains to meditate and to write."

And to my own children, "Let me call you back later. I don't want to lose the words."

Those who love me are delighted rather than offended by the new Gloria. They call and begin their conversation with, "I'm not going to talk long. I can hear in your voice you're busy." But they are certain enough of the availability of cuttings to feel comfortable saying, "I must talk to you now." "Hold on," I tell them. I leave the phone for the second it takes me to push F10, directing the computer to save my document, and I return, the clock for the day turned face down in my heart.

Who or what I will become in this season is beyond my knowing, but I feel pregnant with the promise of new joys. I do not think they could equal the joys from my past, but they will be joys nonetheless, for as a woman thinketh, so is she in her heart. I think joy. I *choose* to think joy, and by so doing, I bring joy into my life.

I am calmer now. More introspective. More tolerant. More thoughtful. More observant. More expectant of success than fearful of failure. More aware of what I once called small details but which I now know are not small at all. I am different.

Here, I see in sharp/clear lines the primacy of every

thought, every act, every person, every experience to my be-coming and to my health. In my earlier life, I understood this intellectually. Here I experience it spiritually.

I always felt a sense of urgency about achievement, about getting things done, about finding all the answers and bring-ing closure to all the conflicts, but here I measure achieve-ment differently; it is less what someone says I should achieve and more what I want to achieve.

Here, I get things done, but in fuller appreciation of the process of doing them and the self that evolves thereby/therefrom.

Here, I search for answers, but with the understanding that each answer leads me to new questions. Indeed, having arrived here, I understand that living is the experience human beings have with questions. The nature of the questions we ask and the answers we offer is the statement we make on who we are in relation to ourselves, to others, and to the world in which we live. The questions end only when life ends—if either does.

Here, I have learned that closure is an act of the heart opening, not of the mind clarifying.

Here, I want no toxins in my heart or in my mind.

Here is the place for purging, for filtering, for distilling.

Here, I know that any diminishing of who I am will not result from the addition of years to my life, but rather from the senseless waste of self and talents, time and breath, that hatred, lack of forgiveness, selfishness, and materialism make of all lives, regardless of age. My heart has aged, but it has grown stronger. It loves with greater care, locking out no one and trying to beat with a fast and defensive pulse when it senses the approach of negative energy. It directs my hands to move in circles continuously in front of my face, protecting my spirit from harm. As smoke in African rituals that ward off evil spirits, so are my circling hands.

Here, I have discovered the beauty of taking time to enjoy the time I give, with mindfulness the Buddhists say, to ordinary joys of life which are, in fact, our blessings.

Here, I feel a magical and inexplicable zest for life. Show me the mountain and if it interests me, I think I would dare try to climb it.

As I sing a soon-sixty song, I hear the same chords of meaning I have sung all of my singing life. They instruct me in how to work at living an examined life and how to *choose joy*. But of course *joy*, because sadness has no rhythm to which wrinkled hands can clap and to which varicosed legs can dance. Dance. *DANCE!*

2

Fissures in
the Moon:
Sharing Pain in
Order to Heal

As a young girl, I loved the night. During the summer especially I loved the night. The sun would set, darkness would descend, and within seconds there would be light in the sky above and light in the world below, my world of childhood games and fantasies. In the very instant that moons and stars appeared, the light in the middle of the courtyard would come on with a brightness that beckoned my friends and me from our apartments to play games more exciting and mischievous than those of day. I would lean my head against the lamppost and, with eyes closed, count down to zero as my playmates took cover behind cars and bushes that were perfect hideaways only at night. I loved lying on my back and, with my friends, playing imaginary games with the lighted darkness above. As the daughter of a woman who loved the heavens, I often pretended that the moon was following me—from the courtyard to the ice cream parlor up the hill, then down the street and around the corner from my unit—and that the bottom star in the Big Dipper was blinking a message just for me.

But even when it was not summer I loved the night, for only then was the city alive from the street up with motion and color. Again, Mama comes to the center of my memories. She, my sister and I, and our stepfather would go for rides in an old Ford to see the magic of neon signs. As we approached Crump Boulevard, a long thoroughfare of businesses and restaurants whose lighted signs made up for the absence of a skyline in Memphis, I could see a large blue pigeon flapping its wings up fast. On and off the lights went; up and down the wings moved. I loved the lighted bird but not as much as I loved the lighted woman. A tourist attraction befitting the Old South, she was black. She was large. She wore a red bandanna and a white apron. The rolling pin in her large hands moved back and forth. On and off the lights went, rolling the pin back and forth.

As an adult woman, I have loved the soothing/stroking gift of night. In the solitude night can bring, I have space and time for meditation, relaxing baths, reading, writing, and knitting fancies with the threads of my imagination. Perhaps my love for the night explains why Langston Hughes's poem about night coming on tenderly "just like me" was easily one of my favorites from his early period. Night always came on tenderly for me, with magic for me, with excitement for me, with a feeling good about what I had completed with the end of day.

Now night comes on menacingly. I rush home to be inside with blinds drawn, doors locked, and my ears deaf to the ringing of my bell when night falls. I need not look through my windows to the world lighted by nature and by man to know that stars are missing from constellations I once knew by shape, location, and name, and that a fissure has crossed the circumference of the moon. I am terrified of the night.

Who was he, I want to know. When and why did he decide to steal the night from me? Did he plan the theft for weeks, days, hours, or for only a second? Where was I, what was I doing, what was I wearing when he decided to remove the pane from a downstairs window and enter my space unseen and unheard? Why did he choose *me*?

Perhaps I did not draw the blinds when I danced in my bedroom. Perhaps I played Aretha and Patti so loudly their sensuous voices wafted from my den to the world outside. Perhaps I wore too heavy a scent of my fragrance in the grocery line or smiled too warmly when he cut in front of me at a traffic light. Perhaps I took the lighted darkness for granted and, as punishment, I lost the night. I whip myself.

The sting of my whip is most severe when I remember the repairman who came after I had called a company the book said was bonded. A strong wind had pulled the front door loose from its hinges. It would not lock. It had to be repaired. I watched as his large hands removed the door, shaved it smooth at the top, and returned it to hinges that fit perfectly. I remember showing him the rocking chair I had purchased for Mama six months before her death, which later became an heirloom I wanted to pass on to my children and thereafter to their children. One of the posts had pulled loose from the top. I asked if he could fix it. I knew that he could. He was a carpenter who worked with fallen tree stumps, carving them into art pieces that would sell for a good price at an art fair or an Africentric homecoming. He had brought several pieces with him for my purchasing. A carpenter. A black male carpenter. I hired him to fix my mother's rocking chair.

On the day he was to return, I arranged for two of my students to be present; one of them, Chabwera, large-boned and straight from the steel mill world of Gary, Indiana, to pose as the son who lived with me. We played well the game we had rehearsed before his arrival. I fussed about the mess in my son's room. My son fussed back at me. He was supposed to be tough, rebellious, a man doing his own thing, but a son who loved his mother. Our staged argument ended in an embrace.

When I revisit the night, I revisit that scene, and the carpenter's eyes I had thought twinkling and kind become glassy and menacing, floating in something that changed him from artist to would-be rapist. I whip myself.

But I do not know it was he who stole the night from me. The voice was not his, but, then, it was disguised, and the face. . . . It was flattened beneath a stocking cap made from women's nylons, and I saw it in one quick flash before he covered my eyes. In my sane moments, coming more frequently with the passing of time, I know that it could have been anyone crazed enough, drugged enough, and woman-hating enough to attempt rape. I did not dance the fissure into the moon. It had been there night after night for all women.

I have taught this truth for decades, but always in what I know now to be the hollow voice of an academic standing a safe distance above a deep well describing for those standing with me the designs desperate fingers have made on the walls, measuring the steep drop that makes climbing out alone an impossibility, and counting the number of bruised bodies I never touched.

I have wept over the accounts of my sister ancestors raped by white men and with each tear I scream out in rage: "For this, I will never forgive them. *Never!*" I know now that consummate rage cannot comprehend the magnitude of that violation.

I have been incensed by Eldridge Cleaver's confession (or is it braggadocio?) in *Soul on Ice* that he practiced raping black women in order to perfect the technique he would use when raping white women, the prized victim, but I was not incensed enough.

I have attempted to keep some semblance of order in polemics around Cholly's rape of Pecola in *The Bluest Eye* by underscoring the context in which the violation occurred and celebrating Toni Morrison's genius in writing sensitivity into so horrible an experience, but I think now about putting Cholly's pain aside and gouging out the blue eyes that haunted all of the Breedloves, all black people in fiction and in reality, in order to writhe in pain for poor, poor Pecola.

I have asked students to critique Susan Brownmiller's *Against Our Will*, a needed and brilliant study, for its dismissal of the race factor, but I know now that the book's weakness is not a racial cataract through which Brownmiller saw the horror, but rather her inability, which was mine as well, to present the horror of the horror.

I had been enlightened for decades, but ignorant, unknowing, untouched by the horror of rape that removes the epidermis and takes the breath away. Now I preface every discussion of rape with "We cannot know its horror unless we hear the voice that says, 'If you scream, I'll kill you.' "

I have honored black women all of my life for their wisdom, their resilience, their integrity, the many strengths which make me weep with pain and dance in celebration each time I read Du Bois's "On the Damnation of Women." Some small thing I, too, would do "to their memory." I know now, however, that the black women I should have honored most were black women who remained sane after being raped. Had the stranger succeeded in the rape attempt, I would have lost my mind.

I share my experiences with my students in order to heal myself, yes, but mainly to add a human voice to this horror which has not been studied enough. I begin by reinforcing what they already know: that you should always listen to your mind, to that small voice that tells you "Do this" or "Don't do that." I didn't listen. On the night that stole the night, I was simply too exhausted to listen. I had spent the day cleaning and shopping in preparation for a visit from my aunt in utter celebration of the joy we would experience during her three weeks with me, our first extended time together, just the two of us, since Mama's death. I had worked late into the night on my writing, because I had no intention of touching it during my aunt's visit. I wanted to savor fully every second we spent together.

At 1:30 I turned off the computer, making certain to save a chapter for a book that would later become *Pushed Back to Strength*. I would be surprised if I had not talked to the document or to the computer, or to both as I have been known to do. "Now, don't forget me. I'll be back in a month with more memories." I turned off the computer and the light and plopped, literally plopped, in bed, falling in an exhausted state on my stomach. I remember trying to roll over on my back because that is how the chiropractor said I should sleep in order to end the back pains which, thanks to my following those orders, ceased five years ago. I remember hearing an inside voice: "Get up, Gloria, and lock the bedroom door."

I answered, lying on my stomach, too tired to roll over, "I'm okay. I'll be safe. The alarm system is on. I'm okay. Really, I'm okay. . . ." Who needs sleeping pills or wine or nature tapes when you can fall asleep in the middle of a being-safe sentence?

Some pieces of the night are racing around in my subconscious so fast I cannot catch them. Bit by bit, with the passing of time, they stand still long enough for me to catch them, and then I remember what for months I could not remember, or did not want to remember. But with a vividness that remains mysterious, three years later, I never forgot being awakened by my inside voice: "Gloria, you have a crazy imagination. You think you are one of the victims in *Jagged Edge*." I was so intrigued by the tightly woven mystery of the film that I watched it twice in search of early clues about the identity of the rapist who murdered with a jagged knife. I should have been too frightened by the horror of rape to watch it through a first viewing. I wasn't, and perhaps that is why the night happened.

I remember feeling that my hands were tied and a jagged-edge knife was pressed against my throat. "My god but media is some powerful," my inside voice said.

I heard a voice that was not mine: "If you scream, I'll cut

your throat." The flattened face in *Jagged Edge* never spoke. I shifted in my sleep. It was then I felt the body and the knife and knew from the pulling that my wrists were tied. I screamed an inhuman sound. It was . . . it was a gurgling sound, a guttural sound, the sound of a moan in a deep cavern, the sound of breath being sucked from the body. I screamed from a place that has no air, no light, no shape, no dimensions. I screamed from the very abyss of terror. I screamed in a way that only those in consummate dread can scream and only those in consummate dread can hear.

"Oh, so you're gonna be like that?" he said, pulling the rope and pressing the knife against my throat to let me know that it was real, metal and jagged. He taunted me, calling me names I remember and sometimes do not remember. He would kill me. Then. That very second because I was "like that."

The voice that came from the abyss pleaded with him. "Don't kill me. Please don't kill me." Had I ever told students that's what rape victims say? That they plead for their lives? That they are deferential to those who hold them down? That they say "please" and "sir." Did I tell them that pleading is as humiliating as the rape attempt is frightening? I could not have told them any of this because then I knew only the statistics of rape which are cold and therefore have no human pulse, no sweaty palms, no shortness of breath or lack of breath, no voice pleading for life. I now see a new horror in the horror African women experienced on slave ships that rode the waters that moaned. They could not scream, could not plead for mercy, in a language their violators understood.

To scream, to know that you are heard, is the only right the violator has not taken from you.

Cooperate. He asked me to cooperate with his violation of me and I called him "sir." I wanted to tell him that I am a good woman, that I love our people, that I do volunteer service, that I don't male-bash, that I understand what a hard time "they" have. But *he* wasn't the victim. I was, and to save my life, I sought to cooperate. Three years hence, I hate the sound of the voice that awakes me in nightmares: "Please don't kill me. I'll cooperate, sir. Just don't kill me. Please." I don't remember that line in books about rape.

His orders were simple. I was to roll over on my back. But the how of my rolling over was not simple. From my right to my left, he insisted. He demanded. The opposite direction would have posed a problem for him. He had to keep his hands on the rope which kept my wrists tied. "From right to left," he shouted. In a weak voice that shames me still and probably will shame me for the rest of my days, I promised to roll over as he ordered—from my right to my left. As I concentrated to follow his orders, I kept thinking of all the people I had called "friend." Surely they could feel me reaching toward them. Surely someone I loved knew I was in danger, knew I was alone in my small bedroom with a maniac whose weight each second became so heavy I thought my back would break into tiny pieces. I did not cry. I could not cry because I was concentrating on which side of my body was right and which was left. Confused, I made an effort to roll over (how I do hate myself), but in the wrong direction. His rage was sharper than the jagged-edge knife. The breath went out of me again, so sure I was that he would kill me and rape my lifeless body.

He screamed the directions again, and I answered, "Sir. I'm trying. I'm trying." I was, but something prevented me from remembering my right from my left and prevented him from carrying out his threat to kill me "right now. I can do it right now."

Details run from me.

I remember being dragged from the bed to the floor and landing, miraculously, on my stomach with him again on my back. In the dragging, I remember catching a quick look at his flattened face. I would not look again during the horror.

I remember my face being pressed into the rug and covered with a towel.

"Where your money?" he asked, making his weight heavier.

I wondered again why someone, anyone, somebody, anybody, whom I had befriended or whom I loved did not know I was in danger. How does this happen? I kept asking myself. And how do you fight for your life when you are on your back and your wrists are tied and . . . ? Where had I gone wrong? What god had I angered? Why hadn't I locked my bedroom door? Why hadn't I listened to myself? Why was this happening to *me*? To *ME!*

I was deferential again. I called him "sir" and told him where he could find my money, my purse, encouraging him, pleading with him, to take all of it. A second time I angered him. I had no money.

"Two goddamn dollars." He repeated the phrase several

times, his anger rising. Two dollars because I had recently returned from a summer workshop at New York University. Two dollars because I was spending from traveler's checks. Two dollars because I had been so busy writing and cleaning and preparing for the celebration with my aunt that I had not taken time to go to the bank. Two dollars.

But how did he know I had only two dollars? The realization that he had been inside my apartment, searching through my world before he bounded onto my back pulled from the abyss that inhuman sound I had made when the horror began.

I lied to him. I had more money downstairs. Where? He had checked already. It's in a secret place, I told him, that has a code. What's the code he wanted to know. I began calling out numbers, but he interrupted me. "If you're lying, I'll cut your throat."

Did anyone ever say you shouldn't lie to a rapist? Would I tell my students not to lie to a rapist? Had I ever read that victims, held down, lose everything, their sense of taste and touch, their knowledge of right from left, their breath, their respect for the truth when a lie can cost them their lives?

I screamed more hysterically than ever, begging the "sir" for my life because two dollars in cash was in fact all the money I had. But I had a bank ATM card and if he would just untie my hands and let me up, he could follow me, it's right around the corner, I would drive, I would never look at him, I would never tell, I could get the money, cash, I would give it to him, I would not look at him and I would never tell.

Details run from me.

I do not know how I survived disappointing him, angering him, a second time. I remember hearing him give me a third order: "Where your jewelry?" Everything I owned in the way of jewelry was in the middle drawer in the dresser directly behind us. But it was Africentric jewelry purchased from the Shrine of the Black Madonna, a local black cultural center, where the glitter of silver earrings and bangles is reflected in the glossy covers of books about our ancestors, black women and black men, brought to these shores, their wrists tied, their ankles shackled, women's bodies raped with impunity; or at ethnic fairs where sisters and brothers in naturals of various lengths or in locks entice you to their wares with the smell of incense; or in the Spelman courtyard on a Friday afternoon where community vendors wearing their locks and burning their incense are lost in a crowd of Africanity; or at downtown Macy's where a large table of discounted jewelry might contain something for a woman who celebrates being of African descent.

He raised himself up from my back just enough to reach behind him, pull out the drawer, and dump everything inside onto the floor. I could hear him rummaging through the Africentric jewelry—all of it inexpensive and many of the earrings missing a mate. Before he spoke, I could feel his rage rising, for there was nothing in my cache of jewelry he could sell hot on the streets or to pawnbrokers. The experience gave me a new reading on pawnshops that own busy corners in the black community. The people who own and run those shops are accomplices to crimes. They do not care that someone had been brutalized before the ring, the television, the watch, the hot item was stolen. They give mere pennies for heirlooms of inestimable value and sell them beyond our ability to rebuy. They violate in the bright of day and with sanction.

Only now do I think about pawnbrokers. On the night when the stranger stole the night from me, I thought only of how to stay alive. Not how to prevent the rape, but how to stay alive. Did we ever say that some women choose between the two? I feared for my life, not simply my body, because three times I had disappointed the stranger. I couldn't roll over right. I had only two dollars in cash. And I had no gold chains. Three strikes. I lost my breath again in the scream that came from the place where there was no air, no light, no promise of life.

Did he hit me? Did he pull the rope more tightly? Did he press the knife again? What did he say to me? I cannot catch the details. All I know, all I remember, is that a voice inside told me to extend my left hand. I obeyed. With incredible calmness, I said, "Here." It was an unpretentious but beautiful ring with a cluster of tiny diamonds. A ring my mother purchased from one of my Chicago uncles. A ring with an interesting heirloom story I would pass on to my children along with the rocking chair, the photo albums, songs and stories from my youth, my people's legacy of struggle, achievement, and humanity. The ring Mama was wearing on the day of her death. The ring the chaplain had placed into the palm of my hand when he said, "I'm sorry." The ring I had not removed from my finger for six years.

He studied the ring. I knew he was studying the ring because he was both silent and still. I began to breathe again and to think, to reason, for the first time since the horror began. I began to think about someone other than myself. I thought about my daughter and I wanted to live, had to live, in order to tell her that this really happens. That women are powerless if the violator comes while we are asleep. That guns won't save us, neither will knives or mace or black-belt karate skills. That you make inhuman sounds of dread. That you call him "sir." That you cease to breathe. That he loathes you. Loathes you for breathing, for being woman. That it is his loathing of you that ties the wrist, presses the knife, and would enter you in order to tear you not to feel you. I *had* to live in order to help my daughter understand the horror and, by some miracle, avoid it.

The ring pleased him. He had something for his troubles, and now he could rape me. I felt him raise himself slightly, unbuckle his belt and unzip his pants. He did not scream at me as he had in his first order. Instead he spoke in a low voice, strange in its calmness: "Open your legs." He was going to sodomize me. I did not panic, for something happened to me while he studied the ring. The silence was generative and transforming and maternal. My mother's ring. My maternal concern for my daughter. And the invoking of my son's name with a suddenness and a courage that surely came from a place where miracles are born.

"I will not!" I screamed at him. He kneed my legs, and they were pulled tightly together by a force other than my own. He tried to jam them apart again. I felt pain, not fear.

"I will not cooperate with you." I did not call him "sir." Did he hit me? The details run again, but I hear my courage:

"Do whatever you are going to do. I don't care. Kill me if you want to. I don't care because I am dying anyway. I have AIDS." I offered my weight loss as proof, suggesting that if he didn't believe me he could check my closet and see clothes for a woman larger than I.

I was no longer a woman about to be raped and killed, or killed and then raped. I had become a woman who was the daughter of a mother, the mother of a daughter, and, with the sound of a passing car, the mother of a son. Where did the words come from I wonder? I spoke them with such certainty: "You don't have time to rape me. That's my son coming home from work."

"Shut up."

With calm. "He will kill you. You don't have time to rape me and you might not have time to save your own life."

He jerked me from the floor, shoved me into the closet, put the writing table up against the door, and left with these words: "You'd better not move. I'll be back. Goddamnit. I'll be back."

How many minutes passed in the dark closet I do not know. I cannot catch the details, but I remember knowing that I was safe, knowing that he had satisfied himself with more than an hour of loathing and with the treasure of my mother's ring. I pushed hard against the door, removing the writing table inches enough for me to squeeze from the closet. Quickly I ran to the bedroom door, locked it, and made a call to my son who was in Atlanta for the weekend visiting friends. The hour was 4:00 A.M. He never gave me a chance to tell him that I had survived the physical rape. He heard the words, "Jonathan, someone" and began screaming immediately. "No," he screamed again and again, the sound coming from a place he had never before known.

Sometimes it is his scream, not mine, that I hear in my nightmares and, when I awake, it is my daughter's arms, not mine, that remind me how wonderful it is to be alive. A hundred times I have replayed the tape of my rush to the airport two days later to meet the plane that carried her from graduate school home to Atlanta in order to comfort me, to be with me, to see with her own eyes the absence of visible scars and to hear with her own ears my promise that I would be okay. In time, I would heal.

My son's friends, members of a high school group called the Cru and members of Kemet, an African fraternity, came one by one to comfort me and to pledge themselves as African-American men to do what they could to end the madness. They never asked for details. I was alive, sitting among them, and forcing my lips into smiles. They were comforted, but greatly saddened. That a black man attempted to rape their "mother" weighted them with anger and with guilt. They volunteered, one by one, to live with me, knowing that Jonathan would have to return to graduate school in South Carolina. Forever if I needed them. They called, one by one, every night and every morning to check on me and on Jonathan who, for a week, sat awake throughout the night, sitting in Mama's rocking chair facing the window from which the intruder had skillfully peeled away the rubber binding, removing the entire window to prevent the tripping of the alarm. His father and I never bought him guns when he was a child, but my son, at twenty-three, for more than a week held a loaded shotgun with mastery.

What I learned from my experience is the dread decent young black men have of rape—that each time it brutalizes their mothers, their sisters, and their sweethearts, it etches them in national thinking as criminals who should be avoided, who should be feared. The intruder stole the night from me, the beauty of lighted darkness, and from these young men, and others like them, he stole their right to be respected as decent men and their ability to prevent the pain their sisters suffer. Their tears for me and other black women were mixed with tears for their gender/race as well.

I learned also that Jonathan was blessed among the group. I had been spared the brutal entering. The mother of a friend had not. Never should we judge. Never. I had judged the young man for not sticking it out with a project he had begun in Washington, D.C. When the going got tough, I thought, he came home. Just pulled up stakes in D.C. and came home. Only after my trauma with the attempted rape did I learn that he gave up his dream in D.C. in order to comfort his mother after the horror of a rape. Never should we judge. I had always loved this friend of my son's. Now I love him even more.

My daughter's friends talked less about the attempted rape than the young men, and I understood their reticence. After all, women live daily with the fear of rape or attempted rape, and perhaps more than a few of them had experienced "date rape." Then, too, my son and my daughter responded differently to their sharing of the horror with their friends.

Jonathan, in a fit of rage, gathered his friends for my protection and for a very heavy sermon, I learned much later about the need for men to speak out, to effect change. Monica, immersed in fear, kept her friends at arms' length from the horror, protecting my privacy and preventing herself from plunging into hysteria. As a result, what little her friends knew came not from her, but from others tapped into the Atlanta University Center grapevine. Their eyes asked questions they did not dare ask Monica and certainly not me: "How did it happen?" "How did you survive?" "Do you hate men?" One eye-question in particular caused me concern: "Are you telling the truth? Did he really leave without raping you?" The pendulum of interpretations would swing on any day of the week from "He raped her" to "He didn't rape her," the former supported by the certainty that I am too proud to admit to total victimization and the latter by my visibility at all the events I am required to attend.

He didn't rape me physically, but he raped me spiritually. Did I ever discuss rape and attempted rape in my women's studies classes? When rejecting the Western concept of duality of soul and body, did I ever think about the difference between rape of the body and rape of the soul? Are they different? Of course they are. The women who are raped, and always brutally because rape is always brutal, are far more victimized than I, but there is a point on the continuum of horror where together we cling to life. Once in the hands of a rapist who binds your hands and presses the knife against your neck, who presses the weight of his body against your own, you are raped. Did we ever talk about that in my classes?

Once we had gasped at the statistics of rape, did we discuss the aftershocks which, for me, were often as terrifying as the incident itself and more than a few times more terrifying? In one, he raped me. In another, he cut my throat before raping me. In still another, he cut my throat after raping me. In yet another, he stood over me, with eyes bulging from the flattened face. Should I tell students the gory details? Is that tasteless? I struggle with how much of the horror I should share with them. Always I struggle, wanting to teach, to enlighten, to remove the ignorance without robbing them of the night.

Do I tell them about the many women who have sought me out to tell me about their horror? One by one they came within weeks after the incident, some of them strangers, others I have known for years. Some had been raped by strangers and others by "dates," two of whom were men of standing and status in the black community. I found myself a member of an unbelievably large group which included women of various ages, body sizes, complexions, and professions. None had worn a too-short outfit, none had said "no" teasingly, none had invited rape, and only one had told. As a colleague in North Carolina told me two years later in a discussion of violence against women, "Rape is such a common experience for women that in the course of one year in graduate school, every *one* [her emphasis] of my women friends had been raped. Black women, Latina women, Asian women, white women."

Do I tell my students about the unexpected pain created by women you had considered friends, sisters, sister-daughters, spiritual kin? Given the bonding you have with them, you expect the most comforting embrace from these women, but in some cases it does not come. They know about your horror, and yet they say nothing. In their silence, you feel the pressure of a different knife. "If they cared . . ." I found myself saying, but perhaps their caring is so deep they do not know how to express it. Do not judge, I tell myself. Do not judge harshly.

My nightmares are not as terrifying or as frequent as they once were. Talking has helped, but there are yet times when I lose my breath at the thought of someone expressing sympathy or asking questions. Sometimes I do not admit even to myself that I was almost a victim of rape.

Meditation has helped.

Reading has helped.

Stretching toward more spirituality has helped.

And even a bit of levity has helped—that is, when I am in one of my talking-to-heal-and-to-inform moods. Levity? No chance, you say? Needed, I say, to keep my listeners from jumping out of their very skins when the horror has a human voice.

> *"Listen, be prepared. Whatever you do, don't go to bed without money. Having only two dollars almost cost me my life. So make sure you have cash, on hand, for the would-be rapist. Leave it on the dresser with a note."*
>
> *Laughter. Nervous.*
>
> *"If you play music before you go to bed, whatever you do,* don't, *I repeat,* DON'T *play Aretha or Patti. Play . . .*

(pause for effect). Play 'Amazing Grace' or something like that."

Nervous laughter.

"How many of you have gold chains? I mean real gold chains?" No hands. "Well, buy you one. Buy you one good-looking real gold chain and before you go to bed, leave it on the dresser for the would-be rapist. With a note."

Laughter.

It's real. Women know it is real. One by one, women said, "I live with that nightmare."

I never did. I didn't think I was immune or undesirable (because it's not about desire; it's about consummate loathing). I just never thought about it, never let it enter my world of possibility or probability, never feared it. Perhaps that is why it almost happened to me. I was too academic in my approach to rape and too arrogant, or vain, in my ownership of the night. I danced for myself in the moon that followed me, never stopping to see fissures that shattered the night for hundreds of thousands of women.

There is a side of me that is grateful for the theft because it has bonded me with every woman who walks the face of the earth; because it has given me consummate respect for, humbling me in the presence of, women who remained sane and functioning after being physically raped; and because it has prevented me from pretending to know, even intellectually, that about which, even with the facts, I am ignorant. I will never again attempt to speak for any group of which I am not a bona fide member. Something is lost in the translation.

I heard the news that "he" had been caught. Friends called: "Watch the six o'clock news," they said. I turned on the television. Monica said, "Mom, don't watch. Don't watch." I put my hands over my eyes as I listened to the anchor reading the teletape about attacks on women in a West End neighborhood. Monica did not trust me *not* to look. She stood in front of the small screen, and she said again, "Mom, don't watch." How strange to have his face inches away from mine and not see it. I wanted him to see mine in the full light of day, to see my body sitting tall on a sofa, fully dressed and protected by my daughter's love. I wanted him to see the face that asked the question "Why?" and the question that, even today, I am ashamed to have asked: "Why *me*?" How odd I felt hearing the nightmare of hours reduced to a ten-second sound bite!

The neighbor who knew the carpenter called: "It wasn't him," he said. Relief! A day later, uncertainty. He was not the intruder, but knowing how to enter my space, perhaps he had drawn the map. Like battered women, victims of rape or attempted rape drink an acid mixture of pain and guilt.

Most nights, I can sleep with the lights off, a great loss to the utilities company, and most nights I have no nightmares. I am healing. I can stand in a grocery line without putting a flattened face on every man I see and idle at a traffic light without fearing that when the light turns green, he will follow me. I no longer scream when someone touches me on the shoulder in the bright of day, and I no longer badger my daughter with a hundred and one tips on how not to be a victim of rape, all of which at one time seemed to recommend withdrawing from life. I am better, much better. Healed, not fully recovered. But I am saddened by the realization that, for years, I have deluded myself into believing I am pacifist, a woman opposed to war and to any deliberate act of violence. I now know that I *can* kill. Any man who attempted to rape my daughter I *would* kill. With my bare hands, I would kill.

3

Fighting My Homophobia: An Essay of Gratitude for My Students

I have no sharpened fat pencils, no smiling-face tablet, and no lunchbox covered with the yellow brick road, but at the opening of school each year, I am like the child who places all three items on her bedroom dresser in preparation for her first day in school. I can't wait for the new experience. I toss and turn in excitement, in anticipation of another new beginning for me, and in gratitude for the people in my life who inspired me to teach.

I am lucky enough to find a parking space behind the building in which my office is located and luckier still to be arriving at the same time as colleagues with whom I am bonded. "How was your summer?" we ask one another. "Are you ready for the semester?" We are ready. We are where we want to be and doing what we want to do with our lives. Teaching and being taught by young black women.

It makes good health sense to walk from the ground floor to the second floor, but I take the elevator and there in the cramped space, our shoulders angled to make room for one more student or one more staff member or one more faculty member, we rise together.

I have been known to say jokingly, "There's a lot of weight in here."

There is nervous laughter about the possibility of the elevator breaking down.

I clarify. "I didn't mean physical weight. I meant mental weight."

I exit at the second floor, home for English, history, and philosophy, and, after greeting colleagues and old students with hugs, I make my way to my office, Giles #231. When I enter, I see a poster on lynching directly in front of me, a picture of Toni Morrison to my right, and to my left an inspirational poster which says that the world cannot change unless we change. I read the class rolls on top of my desk, fixing faces with names and smiling in anticipation of a particularly challenging class. Some students' reputations as young scholars and political activists precede them.

Within minutes, I am leaving my office and walking two doors down the hall to a classroom already full with students. The energy tells me that my expectations and the students' are the same: to learn what we did not know before we were brought together as students and as teacher, to challenge and to revise what we already knew, to discover new ways of knowing and thinking, to learn creative ways of applying what we learn, and to be humanized and enlarged as a result of everything we experience together.

I enter the room rushing, so anxious I am to be there. "I couldn't *wait* for this day!" I tell them. They smile and some-

times a brave or equally histrionic soul responds: "And neither could I." I look at them in silence, and then, shaking my
head in amazement, I say, dramatically, "What an experience
we are going to have!" Depending on the size of the class, I
will do the symphony of names with them. I ask each student
to say her name, first only. "Louder," I say to some students.
"Claim it," I say to others. "Do you like your name?" I will
ask another. She does. "Well, then, hug it with your voice."
She does. Names, like words, have one syllable, two, or three,
but, unlike words, seldom more than four, and it is the
rhythm of the syllables with which I play the symphony
game.

"When I point to you, I want you to say your name. Once,
twice, three times. You will get the cue."

They nod understanding.

"Now if I move my hands like this (I demonstrate), I want
you to say your name softly, and if like this (I demonstrate
differently), loudly."

Sounds like strange fun to them.

"Trust me," I tell them. "You will be amazed at the music
we will create.

"There's more."

There's more?

"This means stretch it out, like this." I demonstrate by using my own name: "Glorrrrrria."

"And this means ... Well, what I want is a staccato
rhythm. Short. Quick. Quick."

Laughter.

"Now, the key to the success of this game is your ability to be alert, to catch all the cues in time. We're supposed to have rhythm, you know."

Laughter.

"Don't miss the beat. Do *not* miss the beat. Are you ready?"

They are ready. The music begins. I direct, and they play their names on cue. Two short monosyllabic names are followed quickly by a two-syllable name which is followed by a different monosyllabic name which is repeated twice, staccato. A three-syllable name is slow. Slower still a new monosyllable. Loud. Soft. Fast. Slow. A pause. A name is played slowly the way a violin bow moves slowly over a single string. A name is tapped like one stick quickly striking a drum. Someone misses the cue, the rhythm is broken, and laughter fills the room.

"We would have had no symphony," I tell them, "if each of you had hugged your name with the same voice or if each of you had not participated. And so it will be with our learning experience. Its quality will be determined by what each of us brings to the experience, and we will bring different perspectives, different insights, different gifts. Each of us is valuable, none more valuable than the other."

I ask the traditional first-day questions: Why are you enrolled in this class? What do you expect to get? What do you expect to give? The usual. This done, I go to the board, place the chalk thereon, and hold it still for a few seconds. Then I write in large letters: "Let us begin."

Silence.

I return to the board and write *PASSION*. "That," I tell the students, "will be our signature. We will study with passion, research with passion, engage in polemics with passion, and grow intellectually with passion. The wonderful thing about passion is that it forces you to pursue excellence. Doesn't that make sense? If you are passionate about something, you do it well. And, what's more, as you are doing it well, you are enjoying the doing of it."

No sexual overtones intended, but they force themselves into the minds of students, especially when I ask them to tell me something they do with passion. Their answers vary from playing piano to painting to writing to reading to serving their god. More drama on my part.

"Passion. Ah, yes, passion."

A sigh sometimes helps, along with stroking my forehead theatrically with the back of my hand or folding my hands across my bosom as if in a warm embrace of passion. For learning, that is. If the students are cold, I'm willing to dance, sing, chant mantras of "passion," or stand on the top of the desk to get the response I desire—an emphatic "yes" to passion, which, in my book, engenders a commitment to rigorous work.

"This class? Boring? Never! A snap? Never. Challenging? Always. Passion will so engage us in critical thinking that we will be anxious for class to begin and resentful of the clock which says it should end."

I am dramatic, but I am sincere. I actually believe that passion has generative powers that can stretch both teacher and student beyond their own imagining and add dimensions to the experience that would otherwise not exist.

I return to the board and write *R E S P E C T* in large

letters. "Mutual respect," I say, as I face the students. I promise to respect and trust them, never dismiss them, marginalize, embarrass, or silence them.

"What I am saying is that I will love my work, love our work, love the subject matter, love the class, love learning, love you."

There are no libations, no burning of incense, and no invocations, but this is, without question, a ritual. What makes it so is the fact that I am immersed in it, that I believe in it, that they are pulled into it, that it repeats itself each year, and, most importantly, that it works. Within a few weeks, we are bonded as a community, a village, of scholars, learning with passion, speaking and listening without fear of censure, and growing in an atmosphere of mutual respect.

EMPOWERMENT is the last word I write on the board; it is a synonym for the Spelman mission, the magnet that attracts students to the institution. "Claim your space" or "Discover your voice" is the Spelman phrase for our students' reach for empowerment. As young scholars, they must learn to do that, and as black women they would be unwise not to learn, for invisibility and silence—stark symptoms of disempowerment—go with the condition of being black and female. I emphasize, pointing to the large words on the board, "Claim your space" and "Discover your voice."

The four students who lingered after Images of Women in the Media, claiming their space, spoke in an unwavering, but much too formal voice when they requested a private conference with me. At Spelman, faculty offices are like the elevator that takes me from the ground floor to the English floor.

Their doors open and close continually, students enter, and, together, we rise in understanding of ourselves, one another, and the discipline we are studying. That this request had such an official tone should have been a sign that the students would not discuss their group project, seek greater clarity for their independent research, ask for the deciphering of comments written in the margins of their papers, or continue in the office a discussion begun in class. Something else, something different, they wanted, and needed.

My office is located a few doors down from the classroom in which I teach, on the second floor of the oldest classroom building on campus, which appears for a quick second in the opening scene of *A Different World*. From my window, I can see the Spelman quad with its design of sidewalks laid artistically on the campus green. On the left, the sidewalks take you to dorms, a computer center, and a science building; and on the right to other dorms, administration buildings, and, behind them, the student center. In the very center of the quad is what I imagine to be the real Sojourner, presented fictively in Alice Walker's *Meridian* as the tree at Saxon College (actually Spelman) which speaks truths from our history. In the novel, the Sojourner is felled; in my fantasies, I bring it to life, certain that the new soil at Spelman nourishes it and that today's administration, faculty, and students encourage the tree to speak the promise which they will hear.

It is a small office, equipped with two desks which face each other, positioning my office mate Jean (whom I call "Roomie" and from whom I receive a good education in criticism) and me back to back when we are working at the same time; two bookcases on opposite sides of the room; two file cabinets arranged side by side and facing one of the windows; two straight-back wooden chairs for visitors which are pulled from the hall when needed; and a computer-printer component which barely escapes being banged when the door is opened. It is much too small for the many students who sometimes gather after class to continue class, but we manage. They sit in the chairs, on the desks, on the floor, and they stand. We manage.

In preparation for the conference, I pulled two chairs in from the hallway, turned off the computer, and opened the door. Usually students enter talking. The four did not. There was a somberness about them that informed me before the conference began that it would not concern the annotated bibliography due the following week or the essay that was turned in two weeks ago, or anything that had happened or was scheduled to happen in class.

I sat at my desk, one student sat at Roomie's desk, another sat on top of her desk, and the other two in the straight-backed wooden chairs. In the small space, we were close enough to see each other's eyes and feel each other's energy.

"You told us to claim our space," the student wearing a short natural said. She was sitting in one of the chairs.

"Don't you think I meant it?"

"Yes, we know you did," she answered, "which is why we want to talk to you."

Awkward silence.

"Let us get to the point, Dr. G.," another said, her permed hair attractively styled and her knees close to mine as she swiveled in Roomie's chair, facing me.

I laughed. "Please. This is all so mysterious."

"You make us invisible," the one wearing a natural said, firmly but without hostility.

"Invisible? I (emphasis) make you invisible (emphasis)?"

"We know you care about students."

"All of you," I said quickly.

"Not *all* of us," the third student said. She was wearing the needle-thin braids I find so attractive on African-American women and which, if I were younger and if I were not "hyper" ("Imagine me," I told my daughter, "sitting still for eight hours while someone braids my hair!"), I would chance wearing. She was the only student in the media class I felt I had failed. My ritual, my challenging assignments, my Socratic method of pulling students into dialogue, my open office—nothing had worked. She always participated with reluctance.

Beginning to take umbrage with their evaluation of me, I sat taller in my chair. "I make *no* differences in students. Surely you can't say that I do." Had I unknowingly dismissed, marginalized, embarrassed, or silenced one of them? I searched my memory for a class that had gone wrong. Blank.

"But you do," she said, uncomfortable for me in this, my trial.

"Who?" I asked. "Who?" I was on the verge of becoming angry with her, of losing control and thereby losing credibility. Had I not always told the students that intelligent people disagree without becoming angry? "Don't personalize."

Silence.

"Lesbians and gays," I heard two of them say.

I could not believe what I had heard. Lesbians and gays?

"Lesbians. Gays." The student sitting in the chair located next to the window spoke with an exclamation point in her voice. "Us."

I confess that I looked at her, searching for some visible sign that she was lesbian, and, as images journeyed from the sub conscious to the conscious, I realized that I had internalized cultural notions of how a lesbian "looks." Tall, slim, caramel in complexion, and finely coiffured (permed), she was wearing makeup, dangling earrings, and a skirt that circled on the floor. Nothing about her appearance said, "I am lesbian."

The students were sympathetic, but unapologetic.

"You don't intend to dismiss us," the "feminine" one said, "but you do."

"You do," I heard another one of them say. "You really do."

"But I have never said anything negative about gays and lesbians. Never." I was passionate in defending myself.

"That's just the point," I heard. "You have never said anything at all. We are not on your syllabus, not in the reading assignments, not in the group reports. . . . There is not a single unit on homophobia."

"Which is ridiculous and the opposite of everything you preach." The student sitting on the desk spoke again and without the reticence that had troubled me all semester. "The course is on misogyny in the media, so how can you exclude homophobia?"

"You have a problem, Dr. Gayles," one of them said. "You are very homophobic."

"Impossible!"

They taught for thirty minutes, and I listened without comment as they explained their invisibility and tried to convince me of my guilt. When they finished, I wanted to know why they didn't speak out in class. They were, after all, indicting me and absolving themselves of any culpability in the matter. "Why didn't you claim your space?"

"We were waiting for you to give us the sign that we could."

If I had encouraged only heterosexual students to feel comfortable claiming their space, I was a failure. If I had found the courage to step from the comfort zone my position gave me, but unknowingly denied them a comfort zone, I was a failure. For all my feeling-good moments about empowering students, I was a failure. If "talk is cheap," mine was minus cheap. Like Confederate coins after the War, it was worthless, and, worse, it bore the imprint of oppression. Unknowingly, I had oppressed these students or cooperated with society's oppression of them.

They asked nothing of me except that I listen to them, that I think about what I had heard, and that, in my own way, I make amends. The how of my doing was in my hands, and that was the difficult part of the assignment. An assignment. They had given me a required assignment. Not doing when you *know* is quite another matter altogether.

How could I revise the course when I was, in truth, so very ignorant? Would I trivialize the issue by perfunctorily introducing it in an isolated way? If I did that, would I not be guilty of ghettoizing it and wouldn't that be just as sinful as silence? What if I didn't say the right thing, place it in the right unit, frame the exam question in the right way? They were asking me to swim without safety gear or knowledge of needed strokes in unfamiliar waters. Were they being fair to me? The questions developed hands that reached menacingly toward me in my sleep and turned me over in a fretfulness I had never known in my many years in the profession.

Homophobic? "No, not I," said the teacher who claims to love all of her students. "No, not I," said the daughter of a woman who, long before it was fashionable to do so, said homosexuals should be given the right to be who they are without censure or judgment from the rest of us. Unfortunately, my mother used the word "sissie," which was the only word she knew, but she never wavered in her belief that we should not "pick on" them. When we do that, she said, we force them to marry someone they don't love in order to live the way we think they should live. I remember that.

I remember my first encounter with homophobia in the black community. It occurred on one of the many nights my mother, my sister Faye, and I went to the neighborhood theater and, after the film, walked the several blocks home like three friends. With Mama in the middle, we joined together hip to hip and switched as one body from right to left. I do not recall whether the passerby was a man or a woman, but I recall vividly hearing the scorn: "Bulldaggers," and my mother's response, as she kept the rhythm of our switching bodies unbroken: "That's ignorance."

Homophobic? I dissected the word: "phobic" = fearful of; "homo" = same, in this case same sex. I had no fear of people who loved others of the same sex. I wasn't afraid of the young woman, a former Spelman student, who lived in the house that functioned as headquarters and lodging for activists who worked in Mississippi during Freedom Summer. We were talking, three of us, about a drive-by shooting that had taken place earlier in the night. I can't remember why I was there rather than with Steve and Madeline Levine in the McKinneys' house, but I remember with certainty that I was and that all three of us were women and black. I never thought about sexual preference because in the sixties, few of us did, just as few of us thought about women's issues. It was all race then. All race.

I remember her because she was the first black woman I had seen wash her hair, let it be, and, when it was dry, untangle it with a metal cake cutter, our "Afro pick" then. I remember her because she was very tall with bony cheeks and very talented with a voice that would later bring sweetness to a black women's a cappella singing group. I remember her because she was the first woman I had heard disclose a sexual preference for women. She made the disclosure as a matter-of-fact statement that wanted nothing to precede it or follow it. She said it, we heard it, and, without comment, we returned to talking about white folks in the state Nina Simone named "Mississippi Goddamn." The students were wrong. I was not afraid of homosexuals.

Weren't the students in class when I criticized "In Living Color" for its egregious gay jokes, lamenting the fact that at a time when the nation is becoming sensitized to homophobia, a black sitcom is that kind of ugly? Didn't I make a similar comment about "Martin" and "Def Comedy Jam"? Perhaps they were not present on those days, but absenteeism is not a problem in that class or in other classes, so they had heard me. Didn't that tell them something about me and my sensitivity to homophobia?

I wished they had been with me the many times I lambasted black nationalists for being so very, very narrow-minded on the issue, and the several times I had argued with churchwomen who said that as Christians they accept gays and lesbians, even pray for them. "To do what?" I asked. "Change? That's not acceptance; that's rejection. And I don't think that's Christianity; that's arrogant self-righteousness." Maybe if I told the students about those encounters, they would . . . Didn't they know I am a decent, sensitive, and well-meaning person and that I speak out against all kinds of oppression? Didn't they know that as a *black woman* (no less and no more one than the other), I couldn't participate knowingly in oppression? What would my ancestors say? Didn't the students *know* I cared about justice?

Of course they did, but Gloria as an individual outside the classroom was not the subject of their conference. Gloria as teacher talking big and bad inside the classroom about claiming your space was the person on trial. That Gloria might have talked about homophobia in television sitcoms and that Gloria might have challenged a homophobic Christian brigade, but she had not included homophobia as a unit in the course.

Homophobic. Isn't there a better word, a more precise word, a word that connotes ignorance of rather than fear of? But if I had put this question to the students, they would have said "ignorance of" is deliberate ignorance of, or "dismissal of" is deliberate avoidance of or conscious refusal to consider it important enough to become knowledgeable about, which is a camouflage for hatred of. Few naming words ever name clearly, precisely, and "homophobia" is among them.

"It is not a matter of semantics," I told myself when I put myself on trial in the privacy of my home. Actually, the students probably would have permitted me to call it whatever I wanted; but, after applauding my neologism, they still would have said, "You didn't see us. You didn't give us voice." That was the point. Even if I didn't fear them, I didn't make them visible.

Had I asked, "Why are you picking on me? Did you request a similar conference with other teachers?" I believe they would have told me that I had asked for the conference with all my sermons about loving students, giving them space, and helping them amplify their voice. Their attack was, in essence, a compliment. I had no defense.

The more I struggled with the guilt they said I should own up to, the more I understood the reticence of the student I had not been able to reach all semester, the one who in the conference sat boldly on top of my roomie's desk and in her clearest voice named my problem. I had misinterpreted her classroom performance as disinterest, lack of discipline, or fear of failure when all the time it was pain compounded by my doing the opposite of what I promised. I had never embarrassed her, but I had dismissed her with the thunder of my silence on her existence.

"I *didn't* know," I should be able to say in my defense, but the issue was not my failure to embrace individual students but rather my failure to address an injury that affects a large number of people, few of whom I will ever have an opportunity to grow with in a learning environment. My mind reasoned for me: "Would you be pleased with a white person who advocates for an individual black person—a maid, an employee, an army buddy, a grad school chum—but turns his/her back when groups of blacks are violated?" No, this issue was not about the individual student.

I could not design a nonhomophobic course until I took an honest look at the self in my mirror. I did that, and the me I saw was not pretty. I saw a woman who did not fear gays and lesbians, but most definitely feared their agenda. I feared that it would minimize issues of race, shifting racial justice to the bottom of a list of national priorities, if not removing it altogether.

No, my phobia had nothing to do with gays and lesbians, and everything to do with the way I felt about my people as a marginalized group in white America. I was possessive of our right to volume and visibility, to unchallenged passion and supported persistence, in the struggle for justice, and I was suspicious of any group that said, "Add us," or "We, too, are hurting," especially if the voices belonged to white faces that looked away from us or at us with disdain. I believed in gay and lesbian rights, but that was one thing, and supporting their movement something entirely different.

To the confessional point: movement parades were problematic for me because, in my opinion, they made no statement about pain, about real oppression. Here, my experiences in the Civil Rights movement, as well as my grounding in old-fashioned decorum and appearance, came into play. Try as I might to think oppression and pain each time I witnessed a gay pride parade, I simply couldn't. Perhaps it was the lens of mass media (white, male, and straight) that shaped my evaluation, but to say so would be to give in to the coward in me afraid to speak the truth. The truth is, I saw gays and lesbians in the parades to be as frivolous as the flower children I had seen in the sixties having fun. The very word for their coming together to make a national statement was a revealing statement in itself: *parade*. Black people, along with whites, came together in a *march*. How very different the two words are. Free people parade. Not-free people march.

In the march for racial justice, we locked arms together. We were silent, wearing serious faces, or we sang songs about the struggles and about gains. In the parade, gays and lesbians, some of them barely clothed, were not silent. They seemed so . . . so free in so many ways. In fact, they seemed to be having a grand time, smiling, dancing, drinking, hugging, kissing. . . . Instead of movement songs that tell a history of violence and celebrate phenomenal achievements for justice, their parades broadcast loud music, loud dancing music, and sometimes unkind shouts of profanity hurled at spectators.

A critical reading of the parade brought into focus the name which said everything: *gay pride*. Although they were demonstrating for gay and lesbian *rights*, they were exhibiting gay and lesbian *pride*, perhaps using hyperbole and shock effects to make the statement dramatic, strong, unquestionably clear. I understood that, but I maintained nevertheless that no truly oppressed, disadvantaged, and marginalized group would use that modus operandus of expression. This reading, understandably, reinforced my certainty that their pain did not begin to equal the pain of my people—women and men, elders and children.

The reflection of myself the students helped me see was not a pretty one. I was a woman who measured, or weighed, human pain. Black people have no refuge from racism, and we are yet in search of an antidote for the poison of self-hatred it injects into our veins with blunt needles. Gays and lesbians, on the other hand, can hide the cause of their oppression. Moreover, they are not struggling economically as we, and, as a group, they have not been brutalized in an institution called slavery.

I was not afraid of gays and lesbians; I was angry with them because I thought I heard their voices in the national chant "Enough already for black people." I was angry with them because in their description/naming of their oppression, I thought I heard a trivializing of the suffering of my people. "So what is new about this?" I asked myself. In the sixties, students at Berkeley used our suffering as a logo for the free speech movement. "The student is a nigger," they said, and, as nigger, the student has a right to scream for her/his rights. Those doing the screaming were white and privileged and, the leaders among them, male.

"So what else is new?" I asked again. Didn't feminists in the seventies say that the woman is a nigger? Well, in so many words, didn't they say that? I think they did. And weren't most of the women doing the screaming white and, like the students at Berkeley, privileged? Aren't the gays and lesbians who are vocal and visible in the movement white and privileged?

How dare any of those groups take for their own use a word, or a history, that includes rapes and lynching, dismissal and disempowerment, psychological enslavement and economic brutality! How dare any group concerned about justice be so very callous! I was not homophobic; I was angry.

I know I was *not* homophobic because I believed that oppression of gays and lesbians must be included in all of our courses. The issue for me was timing. Isn't there such a thing as readiness? If you push anything before readiness is in place, don't you guarantee failure? When you are involved in a political struggle, shouldn't your strategies take into consideration the propitious moment for attack? If you move troops in too many directions, before you are strong, don't you run the risk of having all of them slaughtered?

One problem at a time, I reasoned, and in the order most conducive to victory on all fronts. Homophobia? It's too charged and, given reports of racism in the gay and lesbian movement, it's too problematic. We will have to *prepare* to deal with it, get to it in time. I realize now that, in essence, I was saying to gays and lesbians, "Wait. You'll have to wait your turn." But hadn't Martin explained to the entire nation why we as blacks couldn't wait?

The truth is when the Civil Rights movement ended, and in disillusionment for so many of us, blacks and whites, I returned to the guarded position on white people I had held in my youth. To put it quite simply, and in southern terms, the trust I had experienced was "gone with the wind." As a result, I did not trust white women who stood at the helm of the women's movement in the seventies and eighties, and for good reason, I thought. They were angry women striking out at man-the-enemy. I was angry, too, but I was striking out at system-the-enemy, a perspective that permitted me to scream with my gender while screaming no less loudly with my race. I didn't trust them because when we came together on issues of gender, we came from two very different worlds. I resented the privilege their race conferred upon them: access to the media, to publishing, to the academy, to the marketplace— to all centers of influence and power—not as much as white men, but immeasurably more than black women. If I had been convinced in those early years that they would call our names when they accessed channels of power, I would have worked indefatigably in the movement, but I did not think they would, and they didn't. That is the point, I believe, of the very important book *All the Men Are Black; All the Women Are White; But Some of Us Are Brave.* Although I was aggressive about gender issues, never separating them from race and class issues, I never took seriously any participation in the feminist movement.

If I didn't trust white feminists, I had serious misgivings about many black feminists. And here I do not mean women in the community who were speaking feminism without the benefit of a movement megaphone, but rather black women in the movement who were speaking at high octaves about women they rarely encountered in their neighborhoods, in social settings, and in the workplace. That, in my judgmental way of thinking, was a contradiction a black feminist could not afford.

Didn't the fact that I questioned the feminist movement, including some participants who look like me, stand for something in this trial? Couldn't it be Exhibit A? "The defense will prove that the defendant's attitude did not target only gays and lesbians." I know the answer. It is an emphatic "No!" The students never asked me to include the gay and lesbian movement in the course, and I would not be surprised if they, too, had some issues with the movement. What they asked was that I examine my failure to examine homophobia as an ill in this culture, an ill present in the media. Injustice does not need a movement in order to be addressed in the academy, in the pulpit, in conversations, or in relationships. I know that, for even when I was disenchanted with the feminist movement and even before there was such a movement, women's liberation was in my syllabi. I had no defense.

But I had had more than my share of racial rage and racial fear. Approve the right of a large group of white people to have voice in a national movement, and we will be silenced. Applaud their struggle, and we will become immobilized. I was in a state of rage over the deterioration of black schools following the implementation of *Brown v. Topeka,* and desperate for a resurgence of a national commitment to racial justice. I couldn't let any other group's pain take attention from my own, especially if the national face of the group was white. I was suspicious. I was resentful. But I was *not* homophobic.

The mind will not long permit us to delude ourselves into believing we see one way when the facts tell us to see another. Once we go there for assistance with a dilemma, we are forced to look at our denial, our irrational rationalizing, our games of semantics, our buck-passing; for the mind, much more than the heart, refuses to play the role of enabler. Hence the difficulty I had weaving all of these questions and my own chosen answers into a garment of innocence and unknowing I could wear with certainty that no one had the power to remove it. I wrestled with myself, knowing all the while that I could not win and that if I were going to be a good teacher, I should not try to win. Love for students won out over my desire to be guiltless and good.

I continued to maintain that homophobic was an imprecise word for me, but if that is what the students called me, that is what I was. Hadn't we said that to whites who maintained they might be this or that, but racist they were not? I accepted the charge. I *was* homophobic:

1. I erred in believing I could support gay and lesbian rights without supporting a movement for such rights. Plain and simple, I erred. If whites have a moral and political obligation (and I think they do) to support the racial struggle, heterosexuals have that same obligation to the gay and lesbian struggle. I could not separate the cause from the movement.

2. I erred in believing we could achieve victory as blacks and as women if we roped off sections of the battlefield

and decided when, and how, the struggles in those sections should be waged. There might be many battles, but there can be only one victory.

3. I erred in believing I could weigh a pain I was not personally experiencing. Emotionally, my involvement with the suffering of African-Americans, especially the working class among us who have no refuge from pain, and, even more so the women, tells me that I can. Intellectually, I know I cannot. Morally, I know I should not try.

4. I erred in believing that concealment is a refuge for gays and lesbians. How can denial of self ever be a refuge? That is the most excruciating of pains, for rejection of self is an emotional and psychological death.

5. And finally, I erred most unforgivably in painting gays and lesbians white, following the old line of invisibility and disempowerment for blacks, an egregious error because gays who are black feel the thrust of a sharper knife and lesbians who are black feel the sharper knife developing jagged edges once it is inside, where it thrusts deeper, and turns. Although white was the most visible color in the gay and lesbian movement, I should have seen black as a primary color of pain.

That I made these errors is unfathomable given the primacy of Audre Lorde to literature classes I teach and the passion with which I engage the students in an engagement with her genius, her voice, her courage. What disease had made me localize her genius in a literature course and not transfer what she taught me about homophobia to the media class? I had reason. Deprogramming a generation of young people who have come to age in a media-saturated culture is hard work that cannot afford a distraction of any kind. Challenging racism is easy; the problem always comes from someone outside the family, outside the community, outside the love bed. Challenging sexism is a formidable task; the problem is everywhere, even, or most painfully, in our personal worlds. Bringing in homophobia, I reasoned, would confuse the students' sense of direction as they furrowed a path of race-and-gender enlightenment, or would require them to perform a balancing act we adults have not perfected.

My thinking seemed so very logical and so nonrejecting of gays and lesbians, but it did not answer the question the students' conference had posted like placards in every corner of my world: What disease had made me think this way? I had to confess: the disease was my dismissive attitude toward the oppression of gays and lesbians, which the students called homophobia.

The conference occurred so late in the semester that I could not undo the damage already done, and it is to the students' credit that they did not expect, or want, me to turn the course inside-out in order to make room for gay and lesbian issues. They had too much pride in themselves to accept corrective space and, to my pleasure, too much respect for me to believe I would offer it. Actually, they spoke less for themselves than for students who would come after them.

The students changed my attitude; I changed the course. In retrospect, I realize the asignment they gave me was not that difficult after all. It required that I teach the course described in the college catalog as a study of images of women in the media with emphasis on African-American women. The new course teaches these truths: lesbians are women, many black women are lesbian, and homophobia, like racism and misogyny, is pervasive in the media. It might not earn a high grade from gays and lesbians, regardless of race, actively and aggressively involved in the movement, but I am confident it would earn at least a B+ from the students who took me to trial five years ago.

I wish they could return to my office and, with the tree that speaks our people's history listening in, sit in the chairs or on top of Roomie's desk while I acknowledge that there were vacancies in my concern for justice. That's what they wanted of me. Not a change in my sexual orientation or a promotion of theirs, but an acknowledgment of vacancies that robbed them of visibility in a course to which they brought the passion I said all of us should have. I would testify as a *race-woman*, the identity I believe they respected, valued and claimed as their own; but I would testify without straining under the weight that identity placed on me five years ago, for I now realize that accepting others who are different from me in sexual orientation, or in any other way, and believing in their right to use their own modality of expression in a movement they name as they wish, does not jeopardize my dual identity and need not trivialize struggles for my people.

Were I to brag too much about a new Gloria, the students

would remind me that since the illness is in my blood chemistry, I could not have been cured in so short a time. Struggling against homophobia, like struggling against racism and sexism, is a lifelong struggle. I know, then, that my illness is only in remission. For the health I am now experiencing, I thank my students.

4

A Change of Heart about Matters of the Heart: An Anger Shift from Interracial Marriages to Real Problems

The syllabus identifies the course as Survey of Early African-American Literature, an upper-division course for English majors, but open to other students who are interested in a serious study of our literature. It will interface literature with history (as any self-respecting lit course does), but the syllabus is clear: the focus will be on the literature as *literature*. Critical essays. Annotated bibliographies. Exegeses. Oral presentations. A final paper. Venting is nowhere on the syllabus, but it will come before we leave the eighteenth century or, more specifically, before we leave the excerpts of Olaudah Equiano's slave narrative, the first major prose selection in the course anthology, *Black Writers of America*.

As young literary critics, the students analyze language, structure, style, and voice in the autobiography, making use of information and skills learned in literary forms, literary criticism, and other required courses for English majors at

Spelman. They celebrate the enormity of this gift to our literary heritage, this heirloom, this proof that Africans kidnapped in the Motherland and brought to these shores in chains were not subhuman creatures! I hear exclamation points in their voices when the writer is Equiano.

For Phillis Wheatley there were few, if any, exclamation points, especially when they read the problematic two stanzas which begin: " 'Twas mercy brought me from my pagan land/ Taught my benighted soul to understand" (Richard Barksdale and Kenneth Kinnamon, eds., *Black Writers of America: A Comprehensive Anthology* [New York: Macmillan, 1986], 41). I assigned June Jordan's "Something Like a Sonnet for Phillis Wheatley," hoping its brilliance and passion would give the students the Phillis who dared to name herself "an angel of the Almighty" (JoAnne Braxton and A. McLaughlin, eds., *Wild Women in the Whirlwind* [New Brunswick: Rutgers University Press, 1990], 26), the genius Phillis who was not as silent on slavery as the students think. They read her quickly. They linger on Equiano's every word.

They regret the European influences so evident in his autobiography, but they understand the why of those influences: In whose language and for whom was Equiano writing? In what culture did he grow into adulthood? Whose religion had he come to accept? They understand.

They forgive Equiano for suggested solutions to slavery which some among them see as "invitations to colonialism," and they are kind to Equiano. Kind because he paints pleasing pictures of Africa. Kind because he attacks the hypocrisy and barbarity of European Christians. Kind because he shows how radically different African slavery was from European slavery, thereby making us feel better about Africans who sold their own to European slave catchers. "Our ancestors just didn't know the nature of the beast they were dealing with."

I brace myself for the moment when some of the students will *not* be kind. It will come, I know, when I direct the class to read the next writer in the anthology and they demand another session on Equiano in which they will turn their attention from the autobiography as literature, as heirloom and cause for celebration, to four words in the biosketch: "He married an Englishwoman. . . ." The venting begins.

> *"How could he?"*
> *"Our very* first *major black male writer married a white woman."*
> *"How could he* do *that?"*
> *"How could* he?"
> "Why *did he?"*
> *"How could* he *do that?"*

I could argue that the phrasing in the biosketch begs for this reaction: "Little is known of his last years, *but* [italics added] [Equiano] married an Englishwoman in 1792, had at least one child (born in 1793), and died in London on March 31, 1797" (*Black Writers of America*, 6). Yes, I think "but" is problematic.

> *"How could he?"*
> *"Our very first writer and he marries a white woman!"*
> *"How could he?"*

No, "but" is not the problem. The editors of the text could have worded the disclosure a hundred different ways, and the response would have been the same:

> *"How could he?"*
> *"How could he paint such beautiful pictures of Africa and marry a European?"*
> *"And our people were still in slavery!"*
> *"How could he? At that time?"*

It was the best of times, I could say, and Equiano's marriage was the best of challenges to slavery, but to say that is to assign to Equiano's mind that which might have belonged to his heart. Instead, and in truth, I remind them that not all Europeans were cruel and evil people. I insult their intelligence. Only unthinking people say "all," and they are *not unthinking*. Angry. Hurt. But definitely not unthinking.

I remind them that Equiano was living in a white world. How many black women with Equiano's training, experiences, and exposure do you think lived and moved in his circles? Isn't it the result of where you live and with whom you interact, this thing called marriage/called love?

> *"In a few years, you are going to a different world. Black professionals in white America. That's what all of you will be. Right? Right. Whom are you going to become involved with when the people you work with, lunch with, attend briefing sessions with, and live with in condominium*

villages are white? Come to see me in ten years. Okay? Better yet, invite me to your wedding."

I orchestrate with waving hands the chorus of "Not me."

"There won't be many weddings like that because most white men are stuck back in the nineteenth century when it comes to how they see black women. There are no museums for the viewing of our genitalia, but black women are still . . ."

"Every time I think about Sara Bartman, I get sick. I can't believe . . ."

". . . sexual objects, animals really, in the eyes of white men."

"You can try your psychology on us, but it won't work. The woman in interracial marriages usually doesn't look like us. We are not prizes. White women are. We don't elevate. White women do. So . . ."

The students are knowledgeable about the history of sexual relations and marriages between whites and blacks— white men and black women not absent from the relations. They've read Higginbotham's words in *In the Matter of Color* and I read them again, having come prepared for the venting session:

Data indicates that almost from the time blacks arrived in Virginia there were interracial sexual relations between Indians, blacks, and whites. In fact, such relations were so

*common that statutes were enacted prohibiting them and
making them punishable by fine, whipping, lengthening of
the period of indenture, banishment . . .*

Isn't it always the case, I tell the students, that we enact
laws to make what is natural unnatural, illegal, immoral—ad
infinitum, ad nauseam.

"What *we?*" they ask.

Conceding the point, I continue reading from Higginbotham. Although the punishments ceased, the prohibition
continued. "As recently as 1967 more than sixteen states pro-
hibited and punished interracial marriages." I read, again
from Higginbotham, the words of the trial judge in the *Loving* case (Virginia, 1959), who argued for "the constitutional-
ity of the prohibition against interracial marriages":

*Almighty God created the races white, black, yellow, malay
and red, and he placed them on separate continents. And but
for the interference with his arrangement there would be no
cause for such marriages. The fact that he separated the races
shows that he did not intend for the races to mix.* (Leon
Higginbotham, *In the Matter of Color: Race and the
American Legal Process* [New York: Oxford University
Press, 1988], 43)

Several students respond in tongues of anger:

*"Is he crazy? We didn't do the race mixing."
"They raped us! Has he forgotten that? They raped us."*

Enter the wisdom of W. E. B. Du Bois, whose response to legal prohibitions against intermarriage is, barring none, the most compelling statement ever written, ever spoken, and it echoes, but tones down, the students' scream. I share the wisdom:

> *We have not asked for amalgamation: we have resisted it. It has been forced on us by brute strength, ignorance, poverty, degradation and fraud. It is the white race, roaming the world, that has left its trail of bastards and outraged women and then raised holy hands to heaven and deplored "race mixture." No, we are not demanding and do not want amalgamation, but the reasons are ours and not yours. It is not because we are unworthy of intermarriage—whether physically or mentally or morally. It is not because the mingling of races has not and will not bring mighty off-spring. . . . It is because no real men accept any alliance except on terms of absolute equal regard and because we are abundantly satisfied with our own race and blood. And at the same time we say and as free men must say that whenever two human beings of any nation or race desire each other in marriage, the denial of their legal right to marry is not simply wrong—it is lewd.* (quoted in Andrew Billingsley, *Climbing Jacob's Ladder: The Enduring Legacy of African-American Families* [New York: Simon and Schuster, 1992], 261)

Are we being "lewd" when we scream about Equiano's marriage? I ask the students: "How different are we from white people who were willing to kill (and did) to keep the races separate at the altar, though not, I admit, separate in beds in big houses or on patches of earth in vacant fields? Is it that we don't have the power, and they do?" In telling how we are different—and we *are* different—the students move from simply venting their anger to explaining it. They speak now in a voice calmer than any they have had since the "How-could-he?" session began.

> *"I'll tell you how we are different. The racist judge is a white man who is trying to hang on to his power. We are African-American women wanting our pain to end."*
>
> *"We are not lewd because we do not think there should ever be laws against intermarriage."*
>
> *"Because intermarriage isn't what hurts us. It's not the problem."*
>
> *"It really isn't, and all you need as proof is the way black people treat interracial couples. The ones we know. We accept them. They live in our communities never having to worry about any of us burning a cross in their yards. They work at black colleges, worship in black churches..."*

If interracial marriage itself is not the problem, what is? In every venting session, the answer is the same: The *numbers*. The *percentage*. The *pattern*. The *desire* for white over black. Among black men designated deservedly as leaders—writers, politicians, entertainers, athletes, academicians, physicians, attorneys, scholars, judges, even activists—the percentage is markedly higher than among their white male counterparts. "How many white writers marry black women?" a student asks. "Intermarriage is never an issue in a course on white American literature."

The problem is, Equiano has company, and good company at that. In a few weeks we will be studying another major writer married to a white woman and after him another and after him. . . . "And Frederick Douglass, too!" But only in his second marriage, I correct them, and then direct them to James Weldon Johnson's recounting, in *Along This Way*, of Douglass's response to "How could you?" asked at a rally in Jacksonville, Florida. Never one to be without words that rush to the core of an idea, Douglass explained that in his first marriage he paid homage to his mother and in his second, homage to his father.

The strongest response to this information ironically comes from a very fair skinned student, a premed major who knows that the MCAT (Medical College Aptitude Test) will not include any questions on African-American literature, but for her own growth is enrolled in two African-American literature courses I teach. Bright and talented, she speaks in her papers and in her journal rather than in class discussions. Her voice of anger startles me. "Please!" she says sarcastically. "What 'father'? Rapist, yes. But 'father,' no. What is wrong with these men?"

For most of the students, though certainly not all, the verdict is clear: as a group, black men who marry white women are not "abundantly satisfied with our own race and blood." They don't like themselves which means that they can hardly like black women.

"How could he?"

"Didn't he know how much it would hurt?"

Knowing that we are "done" with venting, those who feel the keenest pain continue the discussion in my office. It is then I inform them of my efforts to write an essay on my personal struggle with "the problem." They loose their tongues, so much there is they want to say and rare are their chances to be heard outside our world, for when investigative reporters take steno pads and cameras to college campuses, they forget that we exist. Whether the topic is interracial relationships, a resurgence of racism, a backlash against feminism, the Gulf War, the Cuban crisis, the Middle East conflict, famine in Africa, or misogyny in America, students at Spelman College and other historically black institutions of higher learning have very definite opinions that reflect very careful thought. I understood, then, why the students talked openly, interrupting their thoughts with an occasional "Put that in the essay, Dr. G."

"It hurts," one student said. "When I see a black man with a white woman, I think that I have not measured up. That something is lacking in me. I mean, I wonder can we ever do enough."

"Enough for what?"

"To be wanted, desired, loved."

Objection!

"That is not my response," a different student said. "I see black men with white women and I think they are the unlucky ones. *They* are missing out, not me. Missing out on having a sister in their life. I say, 'Forget them.'"

Solution?

"And the nerve of them to blame us for their choices. If we were different, they say they would choose us."

Anger.

"All that rubbish about black women being too controlling or too sexually inhibited."

"White folks think we are out there sexually, but black men married to white women say we are inhibited. We can't win."

Agreement.

"But that wasn't Richard Wright's excuse. He said we weren't interested in ideas. All we wanted was a house with a picket fence. He called us materialistic."

They have read Fabre's or Webb's biography of Wright or Margaret Walker's study shaped by personal experiences with his "demonic genius."

"What kind of excuse could Wright have? He married two white women. That really hurts because I love his literature."

Disappointment.

"You know who shocked me the most?"

Silence asking "Who?"

"Diop."

"What! Don't tell me Diop was married to a white woman! Not the Diop who returned us to ancient Egypt?"

"*That* Diop."

Disbelief.

"But that's really rather common for Senegalese men," said a student recently back from a year of study abroad.

"And other African men."

"Even early Pan-Africanists married white women."

"The lesson in this for us is, 'Stop the loyalty madness.' It's time we married white."

"Could you do that?"

"Yes, and I wouldn't feel the need to answer to anybody. It's so hard to find black men who treat us right, if we find a decent white man, why not? Put that in your essay, Dr. G."

"But black men have such fragile egos and . . ."

"Yeah, but they oughta get over it. Get a life."

She is cocoa mixed with a dash of cream.

"Maybe if they treated us better. . . . I agree with _____. There are so many problems in our relationships with black men that . . . Yes, I think we should go wherever we find love."

"There's never a simple answer for us about *anything*. Never. You know, deep in the recesses of our mind, we doubt that we are pretty enough. It's the power of the outside over the beauty of the inside."

Her face is a circle of smooth caramel.

"We are socialized to be timid, to be unsure of ourselves, and one of the reasons Spelman is good for me is that it undoes this socialization."

"But the fantasy of the white woman is real, and every black woman is second best to the fantasy."

She wears the yellow of butterscotch.

"We grow up feeling not pretty, not good enough, not wanted. Feeling invisible, feeling the need to change ourselves in order to be accepted. Acceptable. And it's more than just about cosmetics. We feel pain at the deepest level."

One student laments that her older brother dates only white women and another that her grandfather left his wife for a white woman. A third laughs nervously when she reports a family conversation in which the men were told, jokingly and yet with a degree of seriousness that troubled her, "Get yourself a Latina woman." A fourth remembers her disbelief when a male friend said, "Puerto Rican women are some fine."

Pain.

I hear it again when a student in a seminar on black autobiography gives an oral review of Chester Himes's *A Quality of Hurt* and *My Life of Absurdity*. I want to scream at Himes for his hatred of black women and his obsession with Alva, a white woman, but I muffle my scream with questions about Himes's family, about deep wounds that bleed in the pages of his autobiographical novel, *The Third Generation*. What African-American, regardless of gender, has not incurred racial wounds?, and when does this pain not in some way connect to issues of sex? Rarely, if ever, Calvin Hernton posited in *Sex and Racism in America*, the first definitive study of "the problem" and twenty years later one that asks, and answers, the tough questions.

Pain.

A week later, I read the journal of a student who had been

relatively silent during the venting session. The centerpiece is an ad for Jordache jeans in which a dark-skinned black man kneels before a blonde woman, unzipping her Jordache jeans. The ad was a large poster, in color no less, that was thumb-tacked to her boyfriend's wall. It was a sexist ad, the student admits, pointing out the objectification of women, but she could not see gender without also seeing race, or seeing race first. She wrote, "I felt that someone was stealing something that was mine. Truth be told, I thought if my boyfriend put the picture on his wall, he'd kneel down to the white woman." The brief entry ended: "That angered me." The student wanted me to include her feelings in my essay. That so many of them were anxious to share their thoughts and feelings beyond the classroom and the office made me more keenly aware than ever before that a book giving students at historically black colleges a voice on issues in their reality is long overdue. This is not that book, does not pretend to be that book, cannot be that book, for that is a book only the students can author and edit.

Pain. Anger. Anger. Pain.

I see the venting session as a blood-letting which restores the students' health as young scholars, for once it is over, they close the book on the personal and plunge deep into the liter-ature. One time is all they need. Just one time to vent. During the remainder of the semester, they might, sarcastically, say, "Another one?" or "Him, too?" but not "How *could* he?" or "Why?"

I believe such honest sessions are more likely to take place in classrooms at historically black institutions than elsewhere. That is not to suggest, however, that the question isn't raised at white institutions. It is and, interestingly, during class sessions more often by whites than by blacks, or so it has been in my experience. There was no bite in the voice, only in the words which came from a white male at the end of our analysis of Equiano's autobiography in an African-American literature course at a southern, white, and prestigious university: "He's so high on Africa, I was really surprised to read that he married a white woman." There were no takers among African-American students, so reluctant were they in the predominantly white environment to show their scars and so afraid were they that a feigned defense of Equiano's right to marry whom he chose would bring a response they could not easily handle: "But why do so many other black male writers do the same thing?"

That this fact is public information explains, I believe, why our anger is often mixed with shame. That is what I have been told by more than a few black students matriculating at white institutions. Whites see. Whites know. Perhaps whites laugh. When a white person, especially a white male, says, in essence, "Your men love white women," he yanks the Band-Aid of our silence from a raw wound. If they do not laugh, certainly whites think, "Yes, that is what they really want: a white woman." For that reason, Calvin Hernton begins *Sex and Racism* with Gunnar Myrdal's research on the perception of blacks and whites of what freedom means for black people. "Interracial sex" was at the top of the list prepared by whites. Three decades later, it remains there for many of them.

Academics included. They disclose their judgment call

with innuendo and sometimes in a direct question. Several years ago a white scholar, reporting on a fun party in the Boston-Cambridge community he had attended with his wife (white), informed me that all of the black men, full professors in the university community, had come with white women. Direct question: "How do you explain this?"

"How could he?"

"Didn't he know it would hurt?"

Recently, a young white woman at a historically white university in the South shared her displeasure, which was approaching disgust, for a black male faculty member who had no time for black women, either students or colleagues. This is not speculation on her part, she assured me. Everyone on campus knew that he simply did not *see* black women. "He has had two white wives." For emphasis, she repeated, "Two."

"How could she?"

"Didn't she know it would hurt?"

"How could they?" is the question a friend asks about the behavior of other black males at the institution where he has taught for ten years. "Don't they know it hurts" black women? he said, sharing his pain.

*"I can't tell you how much I feel for black women at this
college. They're so very lonely. My white colleagues never
come out and say it, but I know they talk among themselves.
How could they not! When you see a black male student
engaged with a woman, nine times out of ten, she's white.
It's that bad. I want to take these young men into my office
and just talk to them about their mistreatment of black
women, about how obvious it is that they prefer white
women. There's a kind of bravado about it all. Maybe
because this institution was once a bastion of southern
resistance to integration. But I can't talk to them. They
think I feel the same as they do because I am married to
a white woman."*

For black women students at historically black colleges, the
"how-could-he?" problem appears mainly on the printed
page, in graphs, on film, and on recordings, for living/study-
ing in a predominantly black world, black men who are not
"abundantly satisfied with" the race are men they might never
know, or see. For black coeds at white schools, however, the
problem is stitched into the seam of their reality. Always it is
there—in the dorms, during the walk to classes, at gatherings
in the homes of professors, in classes, and at commencement
where it makes the turning of the tassel for some of them bit-
tersweet. Many spend all four years of their college lives without a single romantic relationship. So do many white coeds?
Yes, but they have no reason to attribute their loneliness to
race or to something needed that because of their race they
do not possess.

"We are lonely in this place," several black women at an

Ivy League institution in New York told me when I was there to do a reading for Black History month. They had come to escort me from the alumnae house to the reception on campus, but they had really come to talk about their pain. They could do that with me, a black woman, and especially a black woman from a historically black college, and even more especially a black woman with whom one of their sisters had bonded while she was on exchange at Spelman. In their cold world where snow falls as late as late March—"sometimes in April"—and flowers bloom sluggishly if at all, at a time when my world is colored with the red of roses, the purple of petunias, and the bright yellow-black faces of black-eyed Susans, I wished for them the sun of friendships and relationships that had permeated my college world and the world I see at Spelman. They came bundled in mackinaws, wrap-around-the-ears hats, and double-lined gloves, and I wished for some way to protect their heart. They were so young, so lovely, so lonely, so pained.

On the short walk from the alumnae house to the reception, they talked constantly about "the problem" and about the young men I would meet at the reception. "If they show," one of them said. When we arrived on campus, other black coeds were waiting to greet me with that look we have of communicating coded messages with one another when silence is advised.

One by one, the young men trickled in, and the categorizing began. "See that one. He never looks in the direction of a sister." Or, "He teases us with visits to our dorms, but he never asks us out." And "That one! He's completely lost. Has said flat-out that he prefers white women." The one male involved with a black woman was an ebony Adonis. The women adored him.

The poetry reading was a trial of sorts, or perhaps I should say an execution of those long ago found guilty. "Inquisition," a poem about a black man who loves a white woman so much that he "builds a boardwalk over the ocean so that she can walk on water," furnished the pellets of gas. I chose not to read the poem (and had told the students I wouldn't when we met in the alumnae house) because it was written in a moment of pain in my old life. It was my venting poem and like the Inquisition, it was unkind, unfair, and cruel. But the women wanted *that* poem read! In fact, they were so obsessed with "Inquisition" that I realized I had been invited to the campus not because of the quality of *Anointed to Fly*, a slim volume of flawed poems, but rather because of the pain in "Inquisition." I read, and when I reached the final word, black women were on their feet, stomping, applauding, and pointing accusing fingers at black male students. I was witnessing and had helped create a venting of pain and anger deeper than any I had seen at Spelman.

I understand the pain and anger of young black women because it had once been mine. The passing of decades has not removed the abandonment I once felt when my newest heartthrob on screen, record, or the playing field married a white woman, and always we knew, for always the union, unsanctioned in white America, made news named entertainment, but reached beyond the glitter of that world into parlors, boardrooms, classrooms—everywhere in this nation. The news would flash, and my friends and I would go into mourning, grieving our own deaths. That was how we felt:

nonexistent in the eyes of those men who gave us visibility and voice in a world that denied us both.

I remember in my high school and college years being proud of the black man in *Mod Squad*. He was so very hip, so very visible, so very much an equal in the trio that fought crime. "Day-O. Day-O Daylight come and me wanna' go home." I would Calypso dance in front of the mirror to Belafonte's scratchy voice singing melodiously. And like other black women, I was proud of Sidney Poitier, that ebony brother of tight smoothness, who was the first of the big stars. Something there was in the way he walked, leaning down in his hips, in the way he read a script through his eyes, in the way his deep blackness spoke of a power that was mine to claim. I remember wanting the mellifluous voice that made James Earl Jones brilliant in any role—from "street" to Shakespearean. All married white women.

The pain we experience as black teenagers follows many of us into adulthood, and, if we are professional black women, it follows with a vengeance. As a colleague in an eastern school explained our situation, "Black men don't want us as mates because we are independent; white men, because we are black." We have to organize our own venting sessions. The only difference between us and black teenagers is the language we use, our attempt at some kind of analysis, and our refusal to mourn. Teenagers see an individual heartthrob; we see an entire championship basketball team: "Can you believe that every single black starter on the team has a white wife?" Teenagers know about athletes and entertainers; we know about politicians and scholars. Teenagers see faces; we see symbols that, in our opinion, spin the image of white women to the rhythm of symphonic chords. In our critique of *Jungle Fever*, for example, we see the carnival walk, the music, the cotton candy, the playful wrestling, which all precede sex between the black man and his white lover; and therefore we cannot miss seeing the very different symbols for the man and his black wife. The movie begins with them making such hard love—passion is what it is supposed to be—that the daughter asks, "Daddy, why were you hurting Mama?" Teenagers are so preoccupied with heartthrobs who marry "wrong" that they forget the men who marry "right." We don't. Adult black women all but cheer when we hear that a black male luminary is married to a black woman. Sadly, we do not discuss how the right-thinking brother treats his wife. What matters is that he *chose* one of us.

Choice is the key word in our reading of marriages between black women and white men and good treatment is our focus. The sister didn't do the choosing. She was *chosen*. Isn't that how it works in patriarchy? The man, not the woman, asks, "Will you marry me?" And didn't many of us in the Civil Rights movement, myself included, support the notion that marriages between black women and white men (unlike those between black men and white women) said more about the gains we thought we had achieved than the new laws which were never meant to be aggressively enforced? The men shook the very foundation of the system by legally marrying women the system saw as anybody's sexual property. We tended, therefore, to see white men and black women through a more accepting lens. Our logic might have been flawed, but the issue was never about logic in the first place.

What's more, our argument continued, black women are immune to the charge of disloyalty, having demonstrated down through the ages and in all circumstances unswerving, unshakable—and perhaps insane—devotion to black men. For us, there was no credence to the idea that black women who marry interracially suffer the affliction of their counterparts among black men, that is, a preference for white. Since women love so easily, and so well, often foolishly, for us, the choice is more than likely a matter of the heart. Case closed for black women married to white men because the number is comparatively minuscule. Trial in session for black men married to white women because there were, in our opinion, too many of them who went that way immediately after their success in white America.

The trial is still in session, and because of the nature of race relations in our nation, we are pounding an iron-heavy gavel. We think we can read these men without ever seeing lines in the palms of their hands. We believe we know them by the signs they wear, flashing neon and without apology. They are the men who date only white; who attend only predominantly, or so-called integrated, gatherings; who can't remember expressions, songs, places, or people from home; who make as few trips home as possible; who refer to black people as "they"; and who have a long list of what "black people/they" shouldn't say and how "black people/they" shouldn't act.

But not always. Sometimes black men in interracial relationships are like the character Truman in Alice Walker's *Me-*

ridian: "blacker than thou" and equipped with the rhetoric, the walk, and the haircut to prove as much. For them, everything good is black, or, more precisely, African. And what better good for the nation than black babies, and who other than black women can give the people, or them, those new soldiers/warriors?

But we believe we know them most certainly by a contempt they cannot conceal. It is in their body movements, their words, their eyes, and the odor of their perspiration when they are forced to be in close proximity with us.

Those we do not know personally who shape a steep mountain on the graph of interracial marriages—the entertainers, athletes, politicians, etcetera—we nevertheless judge. Regardless of the signs they wear, our verdict is the same: they marry white because they prefer white. It is a matter of the mind, not the heart. Isn't that what Frantz Fanon told us in *Black Skin, White Masks*? Never mind that Fanon was *not* an African-American and was *not* writing about our unique racial reality in these United States. We dig into a dung heap of Freudian analysis until we locate the phrase that says what we want to hear:

> *By loving me [the white woman] proves that I am worthy of white love. I am loved like a white man.*
> *I am a white man.* ([New York: Grove Press, 1988], 63)

We know about exceptions to this rule, but give them little time in our venting sessions. We say, "It's not like that with _____," or "They are in love, period," and we promise to fight any Ku-Kluxer or rabid black nationalist who attempts to disturb their hearth. But the second in which we acknowledge they exist is followed by an hour of venting. This seems to make good sense, for exceptions in any situation never represent the problem. They are precisely that: *exceptions*. They do not change the rule.

Nor do they change our history of pain as black women, or save us from the self-hatred that turns us into erupting volcanoes at the sight of a black man with a white woman. We see them, and we feel abandoned. We feel abandoned because we have been abandoned in so many ways, by so many people, and for so many centuries. We are the group of women furthest removed from the concept of beauty and femininity which invades almost every spot on the planet, and, as a result, we are taught not to like ourselves, or, as my student said, not to believe that we can ever do enough or be enough to be loved and desired. The truth is we experience a pain unique to us as a group when black men marry white women and even when they don't.

It is a pain our mothers knew and their mothers before them. A pain passed on from generation to generation because the circumstances that create the pain have remained unchanged generation after generation. It has become a part of us, this pain, finding its way to the placenta and to the amniotic waters in which we swim before birth. "From the moment we are born black and female," Audre Lorde writes, we are

steeped in hatred—for our color, for our sex, for our effrontery in daring to presume we had a right to live.

As children we absorbed that hatred, passed it through
ourselves, and for the most part, we still live our lives out-
side of the recognition of what that hatred is and how
it functions. (*Sister Outsider: Essays and Speeches*
[Trumansburg, N.Y.: Crossing Press, 1984], p. 85)

We struggle to be whole in a society of "entrenched loathing
and contempt for whatever is Black and female" (*Sister Out-*
sider, 151). I have been writing specifically about the pain heterosexual women feel when black men choose white women,
but heterosexuals do not own this pain. Black lesbians experience it also, for in their world race choices or race rejections
are evident in love relationships.

I look at my past participation in venting sessions with
gratitude for the liberation I now experience, a liberation that
was slow and gradual, and yet that seems to have happened
overnight, as if while I slept someone or something cut the
straps of the straightjacket that was stealing my breath and,
miraculously, I awoke able to breathe with arms freed for embracing. It must have been a good spirit who knew the weight
of anger had become too much for me, too much, and that I
wanted to be done with it. Relieved of it. Freed from it. The
truth is, I was carrying too much anger—anger over what integration did not mean for the masses of black people; anger
over the deterioration of black schools; anger over battering
and homicide of black women; anger over violence against
our children, our elderly, and our young men; anger over the
writing of books (by blacks no less) that lie about our character and misread the cause of our suffering; anger over misogy-

nist lyrics; anger over . . . *ANGER*. It was a long list; it was a heavy weight which I had to lighten or lose my mind. The question was, What could I/should I remove? What was important and what was not important? What could I change and what couldn't I change? What should a former activist take on as a mission and not take on? What was my business and not my business? What could make a difference in the world?

The answer to those questions came with the clarity of a mockingbird singing from a rooftop in a North Carolina dawn, identifying herself and the place she has claimed as her own. I could see myself flying to a spiritually high place, identifying myself as a woman who loves herself, and claiming as my own a different place for struggle. Perched there, singing, I knew I would never again give my mind and my emotions over to something I could not change, did not have the right to change, and something that was not the cause of suffering in the world. I decided to remain focused in my anger, the better to be useful in a struggle for change, for the new justice we so desperately need. Anger over black men with white women, I sang, took me out of focus.

The percentage of black men marrying out of the race might be greater than the percentage of white men, but what are we talking about in terms of numbers? I began to ask myself. "Miniscule," I answered. There are twenty-plus million African-Americans (actually more, given tricks census plays) and I was sucking in all of that negativity because of a personal decision that a small group makes! The numbers don't add up to a million; at last count they constituted less than five percent of all black marriages. I talked to myself:

"Nonsense."

"No, it's not nonsense at all."

"Less than five percent. That's small."

"Not really. Actually, small is big for us."

"What do you mean?"

"The small number includes the big men. Men of influence."

Even so, I was quite simply weary of the weight of "the problem." I sang about going elsewhere with my anger. Anger, channeled creatively and used to galvanize us into constructive action, is an important emotion not to be wasted. In the spiritual place to which I was journeying, I wanted my anger to count, to stay on the high road of resistance, where it could target changes in the socioeconomic reality of my people rather than changes in colors worn at wedding ceremonies. I decided that interracial marriages did not deserve so precious an emotion.

Weariness was one factor in my liberation; my love for children, another. How strange (and yet not so strange if I believe Spirit works in our lives) that when I was struggling with my liberation, interracial children became more visible than ever in grocery stores, shopping centers, and other public places. In almost all cases, their mothers were white. In the past, I would see them and think about the same old pattern: white mother, black father. Now I see the children and forget their parents, having decided that I cannot truly accept them if I question the union in which they were conceived. And the children I will never *not* accept. As if they are making a point, babies drop their pacifiers at my feet, toddlers bump

into me, and at checkout counters, infants, propped in pad-
ded seats, face me rather than their white mothers. How in-
nocent they are! How unaware they are of the insanity in the
world we have created. How necessary it is for us to stop talking about who married whom and receive the children without qualification into the circle of our embrace. Our failure
to do so pushes them as teenagers into the quicksand of peer
acceptance, forcing them to choose to be either black or
white. Given this pressure, it is not surprising that they are
sometimes the most strident voices of anger in the venting
session and that their journal entries are often the most
pained. That was the case with a student in the seminar
on autobiography. She didn't "look" biracial (but, then, how
do *they* always look?), but in a poignant autobiographical
narrative, entitled "Trapped by Silence," she wrote about the
pain of being the daughter of a white mother and a black
father. Trapped in a nation imprisoned by race, she was
uncomfortable with the "cotton-white" skin of her mother
and obsessed with becoming black.

> *Everything my mother loved, I hated. Everything she did,*
> *I avoided. With everything she said, I disagreed. . . .*
> *How great a darkness that was! My only hope seemed to*
> *appear in places which glittered like pyrite. "The blacker,*
> *the better" seemed to be my theme. . . . I began worship-*
> *ping black boys, the same boys I had avoided like liver and*
> *onions only a year before because they reminded me that I,*
> *too, was a part of their culture. "But now I am BLACK,"*
> *I thought.*

What pain can be more consummate, I thought as I read her narrative, than rejection, no matter how brief, of the mother who births us.

The student wanted me to share her experiences in hopes that they would open the lens of our understanding to other dimensions of "the problem" and thereby make possible for other biracial children the acceptance of self she finally celebrates.

> *I had tried so hard for so long to be white, and then to be black, that I intentionally or foolishly forgot that I am both. After being accepted to Spelman College, I realized that I would have the opportunity to experience the world I had never known, and my mother would be the provider of that opportunity. . . . I anticipated my chance to be my white and black self. I began to close the chapter of my life replete with cultural confusion and open a chapter filled with acceptance of my complete self. I no longer felt I had to choose one or the other, so I embraced both as I gathered my stuff.*

A maternal woman (who is ready for grandchildren), I have always delighted in waving bye-bye or playing peek-a-boo with children I see in grocery stores and shopping malls, but recently it seems that biracial children are seeking me out for a hug; and ever since I read "Trapped by Silence," they seem to be in all the public places I find myself. They reach toward me, perhaps to test me. I give them what I give all children: my love. I am reminded, as I was not before my enlightenment, that the only difference between these children and my grandmother and probably my great-great-grandmother is that, unlike them, these children exist because of a union entered into willingly, for whatever the reason, and lived in the full light of day. That is what the student who wrote the poignant narrative came to understand: in the full light of day, her parents celebrated their coming together and her birth.

At a different spiritual place, I made a new list of concerns that, working in coalition with others, I should address, have a moral obligation to address. Black men with white wives didn't make it on the list. I would be false to truth and, therefore, to my soul if I said I no longer believe that most black men with white wives have problems with themselves, with the race, and with black women. I will not lie. I believe many of them wear the aroma of disdain we can smell miles away. I believe that for most of them the choice is not a matter of the heart; but not knowing who in the group followed his heart (How *can* I know?), I have decided not to judge. Like a recovering alcoholic who is hooked all over again with one sip, I have written my own recovery program. It is composed of one step: remember how much lighter you feel without the weight of anger and the weight of judging.

I have tried to share my lightness with students, but, like spirituality or what knowing books do not include—wisdom, it is called—lightness might come only with years lived. Perhaps it is an age thing they wouldn't understand. One would think this generation of young women would not be preoccupied with "being chosen" by a man. After all, they came into young adulthood when the nation had learned a thing or two (but not that much) about women's liberation. They should, therefore, be elsewhere in their values and priorities, elsewhere being/loving self and needing no one, male or female, to validate them. But that's an age thing we might not understand.

They are bombarded, as my generation was not, by alarming statistics on the shortage of marriageable black men. "Where are they?" my daughter and her friends ask. We answer: "They are on drugs, they are unemployed, they are incarcerated, or they are dead." This generation adds, "And they are preoccupied with white women." The synchronicity of these alarming statistics and the high visibility of interracial couples (black men with white women, that is) is enough to cause them concern. According to college-age African-American women, "the problem" has become more visible, more expected, and more severe since integration. You see it at company parties in corporate America, on historically white college campuses, in suburban malls in the world of entertainment (where it has always been), and on talk shows (though not of the Oprah vintage). For today's young single black women, removing the weight of anger and pain is understandably a formidable task.

It was not a formidable task for me, a woman in her fifties. I don't have their needs and, moreover, I am determined not to take unnecessary and nonproductive emotions one more year into my life. I am convinced, therefore, that my anger shift helped me, or forced me, to look beyond race to gender in the tragedy of Nicole Simpson. I was not, however, unaware of the primacy of the interracial marriage to the national responses to the tragedy. Like all Americans, regardless of race, I knew there would have been no "trial of the century" if the victim had been a black woman or, if a trial, no all-day/every-night coverage thereof. Geraldo Rivera, who will probably receive a Pulitzer for inspired reporting, would have been concerned about the victim, but I doubt that he would have taken a personal interest in the case, seeing the victim as a sister whom he had loved all of his life and who was brutally stolen from him. I doubt that any white man, in the media and elsewhere, would have announced, as a popular talk show host did, that he would give up his citizenship if O.J. were acquitted. Although data document that all-black juries all across the nation render guilty verdicts against black defendants, I doubt that the verdict would have been questioned if the victim had been black. Cameras were in place at all-black institutions for the reading of the verdict, ordered there by reporters who had decided to look beyond the possibility of "reasonable doubt" to the race of the jury and, as well, the class of the jury, but I doubt that the cameras would have rolled if the victim had been black and the jury educated or monied.

O.J. is nobody's hero (this judgment from black students who cheered the verdict rather than O.J., a fact that never made it into the media). He was a brutal batterer; that guilt was established "beyond a reasonable doubt" and, given the mounds of evidence, made him "guilty as charged" in my thinking. O.J. Simpson is a "native son," as guilty as the nation that produced him. His trial, therefore, resounded loudly with the insanities that produce "native sons" in all colors and that make us a deeply divided nation along race, gender, and class lines; a seriously disturbed and sick nation desperately in need of healing. From the different boxes in which patriarchy, racism, and sexism have placed us, all of us rushed to a judgment of our own. The race of the victim and the race of the defendant accelerated our speed.

Doing well in my recovery program, I focused my sympathies on the thousands of women who are murdered annually, black women disproportionately represented in that group, and poured the lava of my anger on the nation that created the tragedy and made it good copy, camera ready, for media exploitation. That must have been the spirit I was exuding when a friend opened up on a pain that, even in my recovery, I did not realize was so very deep for some black men married to white women. "This, Gloria," he said, referring to the Simpson tragedy, "implicates us in the eyes of many people. They think all of us are obsessed with white women." He paused. "Obsessed to the point of violence."

I met my friend two years earlier in a long-distance phone conversation about the long march black people have yet to make to freedom and justice. He called to tell me that my rememberings in *Pushed Back to Strength* were his rememberings as well. He was reminiscing about growing up black and male in segregated South Carolina when he said suddenly, and clearly, "My wife is white." Had the phone fallen, he would have known not to continue. Had my energy changed, he would have regretted the call. I made no response. Only in retrospect did I realize I had passed a test I did not know was being administered.

That conversation was followed by another and yet another until, finally, we met in person at a Unitarian-Universalist antiracist mini-conference to which he had invited me to talk about my rememberings/our rememberings. I saw people in attendance as old soldiers refusing to die.

Hanging on they were, and with tenacity, to the goal of integration I had let go of. Where they were investing in hope, I was digging deeper into disillusionment. I still believe in the dream of a "beloved community," but when it comes to the realization of that dream anytime soon in this nation, I am a doubting Thomasina. How can I not be, given the fact that there is no movement for justice of any kind and, worse, that the obituary for the old movement included national plans for class and racial polarization that now steals the breath? I have come to believe that even in those glorious days of the sixties, integration was a class thing, or a retreat to which the privileged, regardless of race, were invited.

The people at the conference were privileged, but they were true believers in the dream as evidenced by the many interracial couples holding hands in the light of day. Much to my surprise, many of the men in those relationships were white, not black. Unitarian-Universalism, clearly, was their haven in a world where their politics and their choices were not accepted or acceptable. My friend was a mover and shaker in the group and through him I met another mover and shaker who, like my friend, is a black man married to a white woman.

The three of us stole time from an antiracist session at the Unitarian-Universalist conference—held in Spokane, Washington, during the early months of the Simpson trial—to discuss "the problem." There were no awkward starts, no heavy silence, no accusing eyes when we began, and the question was not "How could you?" but rather "How does it feel to be a black man in racist America married to a white woman?"

Pain.

"People never come right out and ask," my friend from the long-distance conversation said.

"How can we?" I responded, interrupting him. "It's such a private and personal matter. We don't dare ask without . . ."

"Without judging," he said, giving me the word for which I was searching. "They don't ask, but they do. I see the question in eyes. Why? That's what the eyes ask. Why? Why did you marry a white woman?"

Most black women, he said, reject him immediately when he says, "My wife is white," but it is the eyes that engender the strongest response. "Disdain. Disgust. Immediately, they pull out their mental list of misconceptions about black men with white wives."

"I am married to her because of a power differential."
"I need her in order to feel good about myself and to feel more powerful."

But this is the case in so many of such marriages, I hear myself thinking. For him, this is not the case. He continues reading the list of misconceptions.

"She is from a lower socioeconomic group, or, if economically privileged, she is angry with her family."

For her, that is not the case, he says.

"He has always been interested in white women."
"Dated them mainly rather than us."

Taking that one dangerous sip, I come out of recovery and think that this is the case for so many of them. But this is not the case for my friend. He dated only black women.

He does not like who he is as an African-American— therefore, he does not like black women.

Something in my face or my body movements betrayed me:

But if we can't get a white woman, then we will get the next best thing: a high-yellow woman with flowing hair and aquiline features.

Did my eyes say that? Did my body movement speak about the high percentage of prominent black men, many of them dark-skinned, married to very fair black women? Did he know I had shifted my interest from black men with white wives to the difficulties of dark-skinned black women in all areas? He continues: The one thing he did not *ever* want to do was marry white. Are we ever in charge of where and with whom we find ourselves? Can we dictate to the heart? Some experts say we can, say that we choose whom we love, which means, then, that the heart beats only when the mind says, "Beat. Palpitate to the rhythm of love." And this business of romantic love might be what Toni Morrison says it is: one of three dangerous concepts in human thinking. I listen again to my friend.

"If I could not have loved her, I would not have loved her." I know some revolutionary-talking brothers and sisters who say black men should make a political decision not to marry white, choose not to *love* white. But I think to myself, what black woman, or black man, wants to be married politically to someone who loves another but politically cannot marry him or her? Romantic love might be a dangerous concept, but it has its hold on me. I am an incurable romantic who believes that people should marry because they love each other. Period. Mix in a political agenda—like birthing of babies for the revolution—and you have real problems. Marriage is hard enough as it is, the most complex and complicated of human relationships, to carry that weight. I remember a black man who confessed his love for a white woman to a "sister" he later married. They are divorced.

Twenty years later, my friend and his white wife are together. They are friends and they are activists working for justice to the applause and pride of their two children. To see the father and son together is to see two men comfortable enough with their manhood and their racial identity to hold hands and actually embrace in public.

"Our children's psychological health," my friend says, is the strongest proof of what we feel for each other."

It is true, he admits, that an interracial parentage can create problems for children. Are they black? Are they white? What exactly are they? But he hasn't seen any data that document the absence of confusion for children of noninterracial marriages. Neither have I.

Children. His boss was concerned about any children my friend and his wife might one day have. The conversation was so incredible that I asked my friend to repeat it so that I could write it down verbatim.

"There are squares and there are circles. Squares and circles can't come together, and when they do come together, they create triangles and the triangles will never be able to fit either in the squares or the circles. Think about your children."

My friend, revisiting the conversation with anger, tells me, "I thought to myself: 'Are we talking people or geometry?'" If he could not have loved his wife, he would not have, because doing so, he was convinced, would mean giving up home. He was in Germany at the time and ready to return to the States, but that joy he would give up. "I didn't set out to love her," he says again. They found themselves together for hours in a train station in Germany. Stranded. "We spent hours just talking. Couldn't stop talking. We found a comfort zone," he tells me. "You know how it is when someone knows your secrets and you didn't know they knew." It was that way with them. "A comfort zone." Not her race, but a "comfort zone" brought them together.

How could he return to the States with a white wife? The derision, disdain, and rejection he did not want to face, did not want her subjected to, didn't want their children to endure. He remained in Germany for ten years until both he and she found the courage to return. His reentry was difficult. At first the black community was in denial: "My wife was German, not white." Then many went the expected route, he said, reviewing the list of misconceptions with which our conversation began. "Not all, thank God."

He remembers meeting a former sweetheart, a black

woman from his pre-German years. He is with his wife. There is a second of dread. Will she judge? The breath leaves his body. "She pauses," he says, "and then with her eyes she tells me 'It's okay.'" He is fighting the tears. "I can't tell you how good it felt to breathe again." He draws a deep breath. "It is that important for black women to embrace you?" I ask. His eyes are moist. "More than you can imagine. More than you can imagine. The pain for me is that I am expected to cut myself from the wisdom of all those black women I grew up with, were surrounded by. It's a deep pain, cutting off a lifeline." I knew that some black men married to white women experienced discomfort, but this kind of pain was beyond my imagining.

Their courage lightens the pain. Together, they are fighting the myths and misconceptions. It is not easy for either of them and in many ways it is more difficult for her. As a man in this nation, he has voice which she, as a woman, is denied. But they awake each morning, he says, relieved that they returned. It is the heart that makes them so.

He wants to talk more, but he is scheduled to do an orientation on racial justice. Getting white people to face their racism is his forte. "You ask them to construct a racist society," he tells me, "and the amazing thing is they do. They know how it's done." Once the society is in place on the chalkboard, the society they created, whites in the workshop, he says, begin to understand their participation in racism. I ask myself how many of us understand our participation in another's pain.

Our dialogue ends with my friend expressing no regrets,

no second thoughts, no reason to explain his marriage, only gratitude for an opportunity to share his pain.

"Can we talk again?" he asks. We agree to meet for lunch, he stands up to leave, and reaches to embrace me. "Thank you," he says. The eyelids are cups filled with water. He does not tilt them. "I feel such . . . such relief. When I discover that I am not rejected, I want to celebrate. Thank you." He pauses. "For not rejecting me." He left the room lighter and happier than he had entered it.

My other friend had remained silent during this dialogue, interrupting several times only to say, "_____ is speaking the truth" or "Mine is a different story." It was. In fact— "Talk about irony," he said—he once judged black men married to white women, judged them harshly. *That* was definitely not something he would ever do. Have sex with white women? Yes. Indeed yes! Marry one of them? No. Absolutely, no. He was one of those "brothers" in the sixties who devoted a lot of their revolutionary time to sleeping with white women. "I set out to get them as my revenge against the man." As "many conquests as possible," that's what he wanted.

Marrying white, however, was never an option for him. "I believed white love was inferior to black love," he said. It was not an option for him because of the difficulties he knew those relationships pose for children. "They suffer terribly," he believed then. It was not an option for him because he was wed emotionally, psychologically, spiritually, and politically to black women—to all black people.

His wife was not a woman he used to seek revenge against "the man." In fact, he met her by chance after that period in his life had ended. She was a "little lady on somebody else's arms" with a resonance that drew him to her, but my friend says he pulled back because "that was never an option for me. Never something I would consider." As if by fate, they found themselves together when they were not supposed to be, when he did not want them to be. Again and again, they were together, each time their pulse synchronic with each other's. Again and again until "It happened," he tells me. "All I can say is that it happened. I knew she was my soul mate." He smiles. "I knew." I think, yes, we do know when "it" has happened. "I wanted it to go away, but it wouldn't."

He laughs frequently as we talk. Levity helps when you are in pain. He laughs, I think to myself, to prevent the cups from tilting. He laughs when he tells me of a friend's description of him and his to-be wife. "You are like salt and pepper." He laughs when he tells me about the time she was at an affair, he showed up, and she told him her "panty hose were falling down." They laughed. "I was hoping you would come," she told him. He laughs until he tells me of his decision to ask her to marry him. The eyelids become cups, and he tilts them.

"It was a major struggle. A major struggle. I remember going out into the night and standing between two giant trees, looking up to God and crying out loud, 'Help me. What am I supposed to do? You've called me to fight for justice, but I love a woman who is white. Help me.'"

He had no option not to marry her. "One of the rarest gifts is to find someone whom you love and who loves you." Full of fire, talented, and charming, he was on his way to leadership in the black empowerment struggle. "I gave it up," he says, neither his tone nor his eyes suggesting regret. "I took myself out of the leadership track." Married happily for over twenty years, he does not regret the sacrifice. Does he reject black people? He is far more committed to us, more with us in stories, songs, and soul (my racial essentialism is showing) than many black men married to black women. He gave up leadership in the black empowerment movement, but not his commitment to racial justice. That is his passion, his life's work, his other heart.

To the question, "Do you understand the pain of black women?" he answers, "In a way you can't imagine. I hurt with them," and the thought that they hurt because of him makes him want to weep. And sometimes he does. "I can't get away from black women's pain," he says, his voice breaking. "I can't, and as crazy as it sounds for a black man married to a white woman, I am motivated in my work in part by my sensitivity to black women's pain." I believe him. "Because I know we brothers haven't made it easy for black women. We got our pain, but it doesn't begin to compare with yours."

To believe that he should have married a "sister" out of sensitivity to our pain is the other side of the bent coin some righteous revolutionary brothers flipped in the seventies. One side is sympathy; the other side is exploitation. My friend flipped no coin; he decided, following his heart. I believe he is sincere because I have seen him at work. When he talks to people, he touches them with his laughter and his hands. Black women who know him trust him and consider irrelevant where he sleeps at night, so committed he is to racial justice when he awakes.

My eyelids are cups, but I do not dare tilt them, 'lest rivers of pain rush from me. The pain is not his marriage, but rather the negative reading of relationships between black men and black women. How different that reading is from my friend's description of his marriage-friendship. Mental telepathy is what I think when he says we err if we believe black men love white women more than brothers love sisters. "Sister Glo, I can tell you some stories about black love that would take your breath away." All of us have such stories, I think, but who reads them? Who reads them?

When the dialog ends—I have the time to continue, but he is rushing, as usual, to a task force meeting—he says, "Can we talk again? We only scratched the surface of my feelings. I need to talk. I *have* to talk." We leave the hotel room and begin walking toward the lobby.

"Those were good questions," he says.

"Not offensive?" I ask.

"Are you kidding? It's as if you read my mind. It's as if you knew what I wanted to say."

As if he knew what I wanted to hear him say.

"If this shows up in an essay . . ."

"I hope it will."

"You say that now, but what if I misrepresent you?"

"If I trusted you enough to talk openly about intimate details of my life, I trust you to do whatever or however you want with them."

His embracing laughter again.

"But Sister Glo, I'm more worried about you than I am about me."

I don't understand.

"I'm used to being beat up on when the subject is black men and white wives. I've lived twenty-some years with the fights. I'm used to them. But you?"

For the first time since my decision to write about my liberation from the old pain, I begin to wonder how friends will interpret my new attitude, what judgments they will render against me. So much for your spiritual spinning, they might say, but let us get to the critical question: Would you want your daughter or your son to marry one? I prefer that they do not and hope that they will not, but if they are following their heart, I pray that they will.

"So what was the point of these two stories?" I ask myself. "What, if anything, do they prove?" I don't know that I ever set out to prove anything. Certainly the fact that two black men married to white women—two out of thousands—remain committed to our people, feel and understand the pain of black women, cry when they think about it, want to do what they can to erase it, and married following their heart does not end the venting sessions or remove "the problem" from readings, by our people and by white people, of such marriages. But it might make us pause before we judge individuals. It might make us rethink giving an interracial couple that look of disdain my friends say hurts so very much. The decision not to do so might change something within us which will find good expression in ways we cannot image. A kind thought is like a boomerang tossed into the air. Always, somehow, it comes back to us.

"But how can these men be so sure," some of you will ask, speaking with the cynicism and anger that had once weighed me down, "that their analysis is right? How do *they* know that whiteness did not make 'it' happen? After all, there is this thing, this monster, called mind control, called conditioning, called psychological scarring, even enslavement, called . . . The truth is they *can't* be sure."

Perhaps my friends can't prove that race did not make "it" happen, but can we prove that race *did* make "it" happen? How will we measure? With what instrument? Under what circumstances? And for how long?

If we could enter the heart and know, would our history and our present of pain be altered? Would our knowing create jobs, build better schools, stop the trafficking of drugs, or dethrone patriarchy? Would it save the children and care for the elderly? Would it jettison our people from the dark side of the moon where injustice never sleeps? In the long run or the short run, in their lives or in the lives of others, does it matter whom my friends married and whom they say they love? For me, it no longer does. I have already taken my anger elsewhere.

5

Going Home Again: The Dilemma of Today's Young Black Intellectuals

We know the rule: only white institutions of higher learning have the power to validate us in white America. The rule does not appear in any written material, but it is in our psyches, making decisions for us, furrowing paths for us, and placing us in our own world in regard to levels of influence. As a result, many of us believe that black doctors educated at black colleges only can treat illnesses curable with placebos, but nothing serious enough to need medical attention and certainly not surgery. Black attorneys educated at black colleges only can handle uncontested divorce suits, but nothing serious enough to require knowledge of the law and the courts. Black teachers educated at black colleges only can teach remediation (targeted for black students only), but nothing as heavy as a real academic discipline. Only black preachers were exempt from this white requirement (because only God confers status?), but that is no longer the case. How well we preach, teach, visit the sick, marry the young, and bury the departed is fast being determined by where we learned our Greek and Hebrew.

Given the power of the rule, it is not surprising that students enter historically black colleges and universities (HBCUs) each year with the intent of leaving in four years for white institutions, but not just any white institution. They want the best, the most elite, the most prestigious. They want Ivy League. In this regard, they are not unlike students of other races who desire platinum credentials, but desire is one thing and need is quite another altogether. Being black and matriculating at HBCUs, our students *need* the best of white on their resumes in order to ensure that if by chance anyone refuses to believe they are the best qualified of candidates for a position or an office, they have proof of their exceptionality. They leave, then, to go east to Harvard, Yale, Princeton, Rutgers, Cornell, and Columbia; sometimes south to Emory, Duke, Chapel Hill, and Vanderbilt; sometimes midwest to Iowa, Northwestern, and Chicago; infrequently west to Stanford and Berkeley; but always away from home.

The direction in which they travel does not mean, however, they are displeased with home. As a matter of fact, Bennett, Dillard, Tougaloo, Talladega, Hampton, Howard, Xavier, and, my own alma mater, LeMoyne-Owen were where they chose to be rather than where they were forced to go. When the opportunity presents itself—or they create it— more than a few will name the prestigious white schools to which they were admitted and share with no small degree of pain the battles they had with high school counselors, black and white, who did not recommend application to a single black college. They share this information with pride—and in some cases a bit of boasting—for acceptance by a white school—and here not Ivy League, but any white school—removes them from the category of "poorly prepared" and "academically inferior" in which white America places students matriculating at black institutions.

They understand the politics of validation and, therefore, they know that, in the eyes of many in this nation, their black college paraphernalia puts them at the back of the bus when the destination is excellence and in the driver's seat when the destination is party-fun. They know that if they make a wrongful left turn or exceed the speed limit by one-eighth of a mile, their paraphernalia might draw the trooper's gun cocked and aimed at their heads. (I wonder if white America understood the jubilation our students experienced each time Bill Cosby wore black college paraphernalia?) They know, too, that when the nation wants to hear the thoughts and dreams of today's college students, the cameras will seek paraphernalia other than theirs.

And yet, they come each year to begin their studies at black colleges and universities certain that this is where they should be, and must be. Here they expect individualized instruction, academic rigor, leadership training, and faculty mentoring. Here they know their race will be an asset rather than a handicap, a prophecy of success rather than a prediction of failure, for here they will be named heirs to a legacy of excellence and service. "Achieve!," "Remember!," and "Give back!" will become their mantras. Here they expect to be prepared academically and psychologically as leaders.

These are not the expectations they associate with matriculation at historically white institutions. There, being black can be a handicap rather than an asset, and mantras of excellence can be muted by predictions of failure. Every year at new-student orientation and at commencement, many parents who chose to send their daughters and sons to historically black colleges echo the sentiments of a friend of mine who has taught for over twenty years at an Ivy League institution. He aggressively recruits black students to the college and believes, as I do, that black students should be everywhere in academia, but we must understand, he said in a private conversation, "Black students will *do* well at white schools, but many might not *be* well."

At a different time and in a different context, Du Bois, who wrote about the mistakes of those who founded black colleges, made a similar observation. He wrote that there is

> *a certain risk in taking a colored student from his native environment [i.e., black] and transplanting him to a northern [i.e., white] school. He may adjust himself, he may through the help of his own social group in the neighborhood of this school successfully achieve an education through the facilities offered. On the other hand he may meet peculiar frustration and in the end be unable to achieve success in the new environment or fit into the old.* (Herbert Aptheker, ed., The Education of Black People: Ten Critiques, 1906–1960, by W. E. B. Du Bois *[New York: Monthly Review Press, 1973], 144)*

For many of our students the "native environment" is not black, yet their parents are nevertheless concerned about the "peculiar frustration" their sons and daughters might experience at a white college, a frustration not uncommon to this generation of black students who have crossed the color line in secondary education. Some of them were burned third-degree in fires we did not admit were raging out of control in desegregated high schools across the nation in which black students were a very small minority bussed in, and, given racism's hold on those schools, an even smaller minority (one or two) in college prep classes. Because of these "frustrations," some of them come to us needing repair, needing healing, needing the distinctive nurturing and molding endemic to historically black institutions. If they enter with self-doubt, they expect to depart with high self-esteem. If they enter with potential unrealized, they expect to depart with records of impressive academic achievements. In a word, they come for the miracle they are convinced we perform: the production of black leaders and thinkers in all fields.

It is a miracle of ironies because, we challenge the rule but do not disempower it. Rejecting the rumor of inferiority, we extol the merits and strengths of black colleges but most of the writers, artists, experts, pundits, scholars, and other luminaries who come to our campuses—many whom we produced—are affiliated with white academia, not with other black institutions.

We are anchored in traditions that account in no small way for the uniqueness of the total learning experience, and yet many of our institutions are beginning to evaluate those traditions by away-from-home criteria. If they are not observed at white schools, we rethink continuing to observe them ourselves.

We say, and believe, that our mission and our history make us unique among institutions of higher learning, and yet we know that our success is measured by our ability to become black versions of white schools. The power of white valida-tion seduces us to try. While it is true that in the human expe-rience imitation in any number of areas is unavoidable, needed, and often beneficial, it is also true that imitators should be very selective of what they imitate and how, if not also when. The danger of white imitation is the dilution of some of our strengths, for, like grafted skin that does not take, much of what works in white academia can mean disaster when applied at/to home.

We believe there must always be a place for students whose scores on standardized tests cannot predict the success they will realize in their chosen professions, and yet we know that our success is measured by our willingness to close our doors to these students. We know that doing so might deprive our communities and our nation of leaders and strip away colors and textures from the fabric of our environment, colors and textures that enhance rather than dilute our strength, but the wind of validation is strong.

In spite of these contradictions, we perform the miracle annually. We produce leaders and thinkers in all fields, thereby challenging the myth of an indelible inferiority col-ored into the fabric of all historically black institutions.

Spelman is perhaps unique among black colleges in that it is spared this blanket assessment of student preparedness, which, translated, means that black schools exist for students incapable of serious learning; that we teach the fundamentals of "reading, 'riting, and 'rithmatic" and personal hygiene; that we cannot change the dress of our founding more than a leopard can change its spots. Spelman passes the national litmus test of quality: our students score high on SAT and ACT. They are very bright and talented. We pass another test: we are attracting national—even international—attention for our academic excellence.

And yet our population is as diverse as that at other black colleges. Spelman women come from middle-class (perhaps "professional" is a more workable word) backgrounds or from working-class backgrounds, not a few of them the first in their family to pursue a college education. They come from apartment complexes, tenements, and condominiums or from spatial homes throughout the country or from similar dwelling places in the diaspora. They come with stories about how they learned to water-ski in expensive camps located on large lakes, or how they learned to make leather bracelets while studying the Bible in day camps at neighborhood black churches. They come with mementos from their trips to Africa and to Europe or with pictures from summers at grandmother's house in the country, which, for us, means the South. Many come with impeccable academic strengths and need only tougher lessons in how to fly as young scholars; others come with unrealized potential and need flying lessons as well as stronger wings. We teach them to fly, though at different heights. Respecting the different ways individuals achieve, we release some students—but only a few, given our admissions standards—to soar in winds that resonate with their own talents and their own interests.

Our students are diverse in other ways. They wear braids, perms, locks, and naturals of varying lengths. They read Jacobs and Wells, Sojourner and Cooper, Collins and Hooks, Giddings and Davis, and the many black novelists and poets who speak to their unique reality. They are Catholic, Protestant, Muslim, and agnostic, or enthusiasts in the Jesus movement. They identify themselves as African, African-American, black American, Caribbean, Afro-Cuban, black Latina, and biracial. "My mother is white, and my father is black" is as accepted an introduction at Spelman as "I come from South Georgia." To see them gathered in Sisters Chapel is to see the beauty of chocolate, dark fudge, blackberry black, cocoa, caramel, beige, high yellow, and light creme. Regardless of where they come from and how they name themselves, all of them desire to weave blackness, womanness, and commitment to academics into a self they wear with pride. It is this self, and none other, they will take in time and on time to white academia.

They do not always choose well the schools that will validate them. Wanting the most dazzling validation, many do not read how-to guidelines that advise all students, regardless of race or gender, to look carefully at everything that goes into the making of a graduate and professional school experience. Their doing so might result in some rather amazing finds: for example, that the four-star professor is rarely available and really doesn't like teaching or directing student research; that the program to which they have applied is not receptive to women (race aside); that the university might be listed as one of the best in the nation, but the program to which they are applying has received poor ratings; that the university has a frighteningly high rate of breakdowns and suicides and sexual harassment suits; that it has, hands down, one of the lowest tenure rates for minority faculty; and that it is located in an isolated area far from folk of any kind. We suggest other institutions, but they remain with their choices.

When they turn the tassel at commencement, we sit tall in our academic regalia as we hear their honors—*cum laude*, *magna cum laude*, *summa*; Merrill, Luard, Woodrow Wilson, Danforth, Rhodes. And we release them to their new world, advising them to pack warm for the coldness that awaits them. That is what we feel when we leave any womb, and we are the womb: warm, life-giving, and theirs. Everything at Spelman, as at other historically black colleges, speaks to students. The buildings say, "Enter. We have a seat for you in the classroom, a carrel for you in the library, a terminal for you in the computer center, and a station for you in the science lab." The trees say, "You have deep roots here, You will grow tall and sturdy. No winds will attempt to uproot you." Faculty, staff, and administrators say, "You have talent and genius and that means you have an obligation to our people to develop both. You must soar." And the sky promises never to fall.

We have some idea of what they will experience in the new world, for the institutions they are entering are institutions at which we earned our validation. We do not always feel a strong sense of connection to those institutions. Letters from the alumni office requesting contributions arrive in the mail; we file them circularly, knowing that such rich schools do not need the small contributions we can give from our less than impressive salaries at HBCUs, and that, since we were essentially visitors, never members of the family, they do not really expect us to sweeten the pie they serve themselves. Alumni magazines arrive in the mail, and we flip through them, noting an Asian, a Latina, a woman, one of us—new faces—but knowing that as much as things have changed, they have remained the same. This is white academia, the citadel of white male power.

And yet, when we remember those institutions, we discover warm places in our memories we did not know existed, and, stepping out of denial, we admit our pride in having earned credentials that validate us, even with our own students. We become raconteurs, telling war stories that are all the more marvelous and thrilling because we lost no part of ourselves in the battle, and if there are scars we have long since forgotten where they mark the skin. The incidents that might have created the scars, however, we remember.

Mine occurred when the uncle (or was it the nephew?) of William Faulkner spoke at the university at which I was matriculating. I was one of a handful of black students packed into the audience to hear a family member talk in intimate ways about this giant southern writer. A handful because then, in the early and mid seventies, unlike today, we were visibly a very small minority. The event had special meaning for me because, as the nephew (or was it the uncle?) reported, William Faulkner, like other white men, often went to Memphis, the city of my birth and youth, for entertainment; and there he frequented the Hotel Peabody, *the* place, which was a short distance from the drugstore at which my father worked in the second decade of the twentieth century and, in the fifties, the place of employment for my uncles. Then, waiting tables and serving white men were jobs designated for black men only. (How the South has changed!)

My uncles would regale the family with stories about white movie stars (all men) who demanded that black waiters do everything but stand on their heads for a nothing of a tip. The men (Should I call their names?) were not always Southerners. Back then, fun for white people was a trip South to the world where colored people could be asked to spin around and jump Jim Crow, just as, in the twenties, fun was a trip to Harlem, where black people, in feathers or zoot suits, kicked their legs high or shook their hips for the delight of patrons, all white. Jazz. Jim Crow. The Cotton Club. The Hotel Peabody. From the perspective of white America, "same difference," my father would say.

My uncles' stories gave me special eyes in the Georgia Theater in Memphis, and therefore, unlike my peers, I could watch actors on the silver screen and offer proof that "That one is mean." Or "That one is cheap." Or "That one is worse than any southern white man you could find." I would wonder when I heard my uncles' stories whether or not black cooks (How the South has changed!) at the Peabody acted out their anger as some of us did during slavery. How foolish white men were to trust that the soup they ate was uncontaminated.

When Faulkner's relative (What does it matter whether he was nephew or uncle?) mentioned Memphis and the Peabody, I considered myself a participant in his rememberings. White students, I assumed, knew nothing about the Peabody or skipping rocks on the colored end of the Mississippi River, but, like me, they wanted to know more about the black woman the uncle/nephew/relative had mentioned briefly in his memories of William Faulkner. During the question-answer period, when my hand was finally recognized, I stood up, identified myself as a Memphian, told him that I skipped rocks on the river (I might have demonstrated with the twist of my wrist over the head of someone who wondered who this crazy black woman was), and that my uncles waited tables at the Peabody. And then the error: I asked him questions about the black woman who was, without question, central in Faulkner's life. Though a bit uncomfortable, he added a few words to the few he had already given. It wasn't much, but the audience was grateful that I had asked the question to which they, too, had wanted answers.

The lecture ended and, along with others from the audience, I rushed to the stage, to shake the speaker's hand and to thank him, genuinely, for being so gracious, Southern style. Four steps to the right led to the stage. I never made it to the first one, for blocking my path was a graying Faulknerian professor/scholar who, in build and in visage, fit the image I had of many white characters in any number of Faulkner's novels. I knew him as the professor who, without flinching, informed his classes that black literature was not worth reading, the possible exception being *Invisible Man*, an evaluation of our literature that, two decades later, would be a refrain in analysis of what scholars call cultural literacy. He did not wait for me to reach him before he began shaking his finger in my face (less white now in sharp contrast to his fiery red complexion) and warning me, his voice raised, never to embarrass the university. For someone who had no right to be there, I had some nerve "asking Mr. Faulkner anything."

Amazingly, twenty years later, I can tell the story without anger, having been reared in a family that discouraged long bouts with anger and nurtured in a black community that taught us the complexity and confusion of white people. I understood then, as I understand today, that the professor was a product of his time and a victim of an upbringing that made the soil of my birthplace too arid for the planting of healing and liberating truths, even in academia. The pain I experienced lasted just long enough for me to pull myself together and walk, alone, out of the white-filled auditorium and across the white campus to an old car which knew what stretches of the expressway, what turns, what exits to take from the white section of the city to the black community where reality was a creative syncretism of what we take from white America and what we give ourselves. The embarrassment I suffered left as soon as I put my key into the door of home, but the victimization my professor was suffering remained with him. I was free to study the genius of black writers *and* Faulkner. He was not.

There were low moments in our experiences, but high moments with friendships we never expected to forge within and across racial lines. In my first white-school experience, I found a friend in Jocelyn Jackson, a talented black woman from D.C. I would later work with in the Atlanta University

Center; Bobby McClain, a black man who would later preach and teach black theology; Bryan, a black man from Virginia, tall enough to be a basketball player, but wasn't because he was brilliant enough to be the finest scholar in the program, and was; Sheila Kowal, a slim dance-walking and gentle Jewish woman whose immersion in spirit rather than curiosity about race drew us together in genuine bonding; the Whitneys from Iowa; the Vogels from Kansas; Peter Dowell from Emory. Friends all.

As teachers, we remember, we share, we advise, we counsel, and, with pride, we send our students away from home, academically and psychologically prepared, to the institutions of their choice, where we want them to go, where they must go, where our people's history insists that they go.

Home is relatively small and certainly not grand in the material way America describes grand. Spelman, for example, is composed of thirty-three acres and twenty-four buildings, one of them a state-of-the-art academic center made possible by a gift from Drs. Bill and Camille Cosby. It is an immaculate place blessed with verdant green in both spring and fall. In all seasons, it is beautiful and special. The campus is decorated with flowers and trees; and the buildings with paintings, plaques, and bulletin boards, the clutter of which is a testimony to the life and energy at UNCF institutions and, as well, to the student-focus of our work. Trips to Africa, Brazil, and Europe. Summer grants for internships in science, international studies, and mass communication. Fliers announcing seminars and rallies and creative productions and interviews for Luard and Rhodes, for study-abroad programs and volunteer programs across the nation. Student-centeredness. And warmth. We hug at Spelman, we speak at Spelman, we even call across the campus at Spelman if we so desire.

This is the home white America does not know exists, for racism would leave unchanged the old image of black schools as one-room shacks crowded with students new to the written word.

The way black colleges market our need for financial support sometimes obscures our health and our strengths, creating a distorted picture of who we are, which cancels out, in the minds of the unknowing, what we do. UNCF commercials with the compelling theme "A mind is a terrible thing to waste" today show thriving black colleges and graphs of our remarkable achievements, but the image that still tugs at the heart of America, or the pockets, shows a young black man waiting on a country road for the college bus which fails to stop, or (my favorite) a round-faced, absolutely precious young boy emptying a jar of pennies in a kitchen with a pot-bellied stove to help with his brother's college expenses. Neither ad is aired any longer, but both remain in the psyche of the nation. Marketing our colleges creates a catch-22 situation. If it looks like we are doing too well, no funds. If we have no funds, we can't do well. Unfortunately, viewers make a mental leap from financial need to inferiority. They might do so if the students in need are white, but a racist reading of black colleges makes the leap immediate.

For years now, or decades, we have dialogued among ourselves about the vast differences among black colleges, and, arguing that the weak among us hurt the image of the strong, we often identify the schools we think should be closed. But I submit that closing a dozen weak black institutions would not close the lens through which white America sees us. That lens is race, not academics. It is also race for white institutions which explains why a hundred weak institutions among them do not jeopardize their academic integrity as a group. If strong black institutions with records of achievement that exceed those of many historically white schools won't give us a new image, closing weak schools won't either. The fault is not in the existence of weak black institutions, but rather in the racist way the nation views black colleges as a group.

Many HBCUs are strong institutions, but we are different from the institutions our students enter when they leave us. Primarily, we are four-year liberal arts colleges offering baccalaureate degrees. They are mega-universities offering every degree on the academic market: M.A., M.S., M.B.A., Ph.D., M.D., L.D., and others. We are teaching institutions; they are research institutions. Ours is, by design, a small and intimate community. Theirs, a large and impersonal world. We fund-raise for new buildings. They have all the buildings they need, and then some: gymnasia accommodating different needs for physical fitness with equipment of every kind in abundance and Olympic-sized swimming pools, saunas, steam rooms, jacuzzis, and bowling centers in the buildings; student centers tiered with various types of cuisines with CD listening booths and coffee shops brewing exotic blends; and private faculty restaurants where waiters in white jackets move in the light of grand chandeliers as they fill fine crystal with the best year.

Buildings, buildings, buildings. Acres, acres, acres. Money, money, money. Power, power, power. Validation. We are not in competition with these institutions, but they are the yardstick by which HBCUs are measured. Understandably, our students look with new eyes at the miracle of black colleges, wondering how we/they make it happen, so little do we have in our world of functionality compared to the plenty of their new world. They value home more, not less.

That is what we hear when we see them at professional meetings or converse with them by mail or by phone, continuing our mentoring from a distance. Without being with them, we are aware of some of their experiences. We know, for example, that they, like us, are being asked "the" questions, which, for my generation, displayed a white ignorance about black people that would have been laughable (and sometimes was) were it not so sad a commentary on the divisions between us, or a white resistance to seeing our full face rather than the profile they themselves drew. We rarely had questions for white people because as a group we were sure we knew white people as a group. We came out of our mothers' wombs knowing them because our mothers and grandmothers knew them so very, very well.

We fielded questions about black hair, black food, black worship, black music, black dance movements . . . and with each answer we sought to prove that we did the same things they did, and did them better. (Did Du Bois say that double-consciousness requires a constant vigilance of self that produces weariness?) We loved opera and the blues, played chess and checkers, sat still to the drone of a dull sermon in a white church and clapped our hands to the spirit of gospel in a black Baptist church, recited one of Dunbar's dialect poems (sad that he called them a "jingle in a broken tongue"), and, without a heavy Southern accent, dramatized Shakespeare's soliloquies. In a word, being both black and American, no less one than the other, we showed off our two selves with vanity and pride.

Having come into adulthood in desegregated schools and communities, our students field very different questions: How do they see the so-called conflict between Malcolm and Martin? Was Farrakhan involved in the assassination? Do they believe in busing; were they bussed? Was Mike Tyson guilty? Did Anita Hill tell the truth? Do blacks hate Jews? Is affirmative action good or bad for blacks? And, of course, they hear the expected questions from whites and from other blacks as well: What was it like attending a black college?

Racial myths, like the stubborn fungi they are, grow fast when they are incubated in the darkness of white academia. There they are a curiosity that cannot be satisfied, an investigation without parameters, a body of questions to which whites have already given the answer. Question: "Don't black schools cripple black students by placing them in an all-black world and immersing them in an all-black curriculum?" I have no doubt that our students answer this question as I did when it was put to me at an Eastern school after a reading from *Pushed Back to Strength*. We could say immediately that since the "real" world is composed of whites *and* blacks and layered in racial complexity, this question could just as well be asked of students in white academia, but it is a question only for us, and always has been.

Ignorance about black colleges leads to the assumption that our curricula are extended Black History celebrations, but if the truth be told, our curricula are as "white" as those in white academia, if not more so. In fact this is one of the broken parts of our institutions that we must fix, but, ironically, it is broken precisely because it was our way of fixing something else—our blackness, or, put another way, it was a way of validating ourselves. The fact is that black studies, soon after its creation, became the province of white schools, and so, too, women's studies. Held hostage by the need to prove ourselves on GREs (which do not test for black studies or women's studies), many HBCUs cling to the traditional curriculum with a fervor, a desperation, really, that white academia does not have, and cling as well to safe ways of stretching our students intellectually. White schools will release students for an entire semester or even a year to study whatever they desire, to travel the world in search of themselves, to do their own thing, but we hold on, knowing that for us such a release would be given a different spin, a racist spin, that is, our students are bypassing academics and having fun. This is the difference between privilege and marginality. The former is free to experiment (and therefore to create and define) without risk; the latter is not.

The truth is that historically black colleges are not isolated from the "real" world (which means the white world in the same way that "universal" in literature means white) in curriculum or in any other way. Since our inception, our faculty has been integrated (which is just reason for white academia to study us as models for diversity), and, though our student body is essentially all black, our doors have been open to all students since our founding. But even if our curricula were all black and our faculty all black, our students would not be crippled. They do not need to live in white academia as a small minority in order to know how to live in white America as a large and vocal minority. Indeed, instructions in how to function in white America come with the first steps we take without falling.

Question: "Isn't it true that black college students are preoccupied with clothes?" The nation does not see our students pulling on a pair of blue jeans in order to make class on time, to spend hours at the computer or all night in the science lab. The best way to respond to this myth is to call it a myth, and move on. But something needs to be said here about double standards reeking of racism, and about a damned-if-you-do-damned-if-you-don't reading of whatever we do. If we look too good, we are accused of being materialistic. If we look sloppy, we are accused of being unclean and unkempt. A "hippie" look for a white person is political; for a black person, irresponsible, disheveled, distasteful.

Black college women everywhere are attentive to physical appearance, as well they should be because they are black and female, and anyone who knows anything about the history of black women in white America knows that the "right" appearance (like manners and virtue) has always been needed to challenge the image of sexually loose or immoral women who were never expected to be cleared of blemishes in the kiln of "true womanhood," or to be able to substitute for requirements of "white beauty" we do not have. The lingering effects of "lifting as we climb" might very well be seen in a neatness that characterizes many HBCU students and other black women in this nation as materialistic, but neatness and looking good (in a suit bought at discount at T. J. Maxx, handed down from older siblings, or accepted as a gift from a wealthy white employer) is one thing, I tell the students, worshiping clothes is something altogether different. Always there is the impinging of duality upon our reality or upon others' reading of our reality.

Only once did I lose my cool in the face of this double standard. I was in Harvard Square walking with a colleague when we passed a group of teenagers and twenty-something youths with uncombed or spiked hair, diamonded noses, and unironed, unmatched/soiled clothing. I had seen them before and had never given much thought to them except to note what a stark contrast they were to students who walked the rhythm of validation within Harvard Yard. But when my friend spoke with such delight about what they added to Harvard Square, an "artsy feel," he said, I thought "class" and accused him of being condescending; and later I thought "race" and accused him of being blind to his own racism. If the group were predominantly black, I have no doubt that Harvard would not tolerate their presence, for, instead of being an artsy attraction, they would be a threat requiring removal by Cambridge police. Racism gives white people the freedom to step outside their own definitions of acceptability without incurring punishment or censure and exacts such heavy standards on blacks that even when we fit the definitions, we don't. And classism gives people of privilege, regardless of race, this same freedom.

Question: "Aren't black colleges party schools?" Home? A party place? The students remember at home struggling against what outsiders call the paternalism of home. Mandatory convocations. Curfews. Rituals. And rules, rules, rules. No male visitors after a certain hour and definitely not overnight. No alcohol and definitely no transporting of kegs of beer into the dorms and elsewhere on campus. Fraternities, yes; but fraternity houses that are mansions in a row of mansions operating under their own rules?, no. Home? A party place any more than any school in white America is a party school? Pshaw!

College students across the nation are alike in so many ways that to talk about differences is stereotyping, speculation, the neat packaging of untenable conclusions—all euphemisms for unbridled racism. For example, when white college students spring-break in Florida, white America, remembering its own youthful college forays, responds, "You're only young once!" But when black college students do the same thing, white America goes into a state of panic. And the troops arrive and the police arrive and the arrested blacks are captured in national media as disrupters of the peace—students at black colleges whether they show a college ID or not. They are black; that is sufficient. The lesson here for us, of course, is that we can rarely do what white people do and expect the same response that white people receive. The lesson for our nation is that the few gains we have made in desegregation should not suggest that the racial millennium has arrived.

What our students learn early in their stay away from home is the skill of white myth makers in protecting their own image and in justifying or explaining away their behavior. Myth: African-American women are sexually loose creatures, lascivious with insatiable appetites. White Americans have not gotten beyond their first reading of our African ancestors. One look at our bare breasts and one mesmerizing experience with our ritualistic dances, European enslavers, feeding their own sexual fantasies, created the myth that, four centuries later, shapes media images of black women and, alas, questions about us in the white academy. In racist readings of black sexuality it's the sweeter the juice, the rougher the thrust, the larger the genitalia, the more party-consumed the school. Pshaw!

Our students might be asked to participate in the game Black College Trivia, but that is not what they write home about. They are concerned about more serious matters, chief among them experiences with professors who see and evaluate them through the prism of race. They are not surprised that such professors exist, for the academy, after all, is a microcosm of the larger world. They are not surprised, but they are certainly stung when eyes deliberately overlook their hands, when ears strain for the absence of depth in their analysis of texts, and when an energy says they are not wanted. For racist professors, our students are either invisible beyond finding or very visible in a way that intrudes, disturbs, and disrupts the natural flow of life in white academia.

It is a sad commentary on race relations in the nineties that experiences with these professors might be more frequent than they were for my generation, and for reason. Then, in white academia, the presence of a few of us stroked the conscience; the sight of too many of us today stokes the fire of an anger fueled by national preoccupation with so-called losses of white people, mostly white men. My generation, few in number, was not held responsible for lowering academic standards. Today's generation of black students is not so lucky. In the racist debate on affirmative action, they are to lowered standards what the masses of black people are to crime: the culprits. A distinguished professor at Harvard University, as quoted in the January–February 1993 issue of *Harvard Magazine*, speaks for a growing number of white professors:

> *Grade inflation coincided with the arrival of large numbers of black students on the Harvard campus; many white professors were unwilling to give C's to black students, so they also wouldn't give C's to white students. A 'C' used to be the grade for an average performance. Nowadays it's a slap in the face.*

My generation benefited somewhat from national responses to the cadence, imagery, and wisdom of Martin Luther King's sermons on the "Beloved Community." Today's generation is not so fortunate. They must respond to *The Bell Curve*, a study without cadence or imagery, a study that mistakes data, albeit well chosen, for logic and presents graphs as drawings by the hand of truth.

My generation sang songs about freedom and justice to a nation that did not deny racism was a consummate evil. Today's generation is not so fortunate. At a time when insidious racism is a neon flashing in public policy, medical care, and even education, they are told that it no longer exists. Worse, they are asked to believe that what is clearly the impact of racism on the lives of the working class among our people is not racism at all, but rather the imprint of genetic weaknesses. My generation heard "struggle" and "success." Today's generation hears "failure" and the silence of deliberate and malign neglect. All of this we read in *The End of Racism*:

> *Despite substantial progress over the past few decades, African-Americans continue to show continuous evidence of* failure—failure *in the workplace,* failure *in schools and colleges, and* failure *to maintain intact families and secure communities. Taken together, these hardships and* inadequacies *virtually assure that blacks will not achieve equality of earnings and status with other groups anytime soon. Even more seriously, they threaten to . . .* endanger the economic and physical integrity of society as a whole. *(emphasis mine),* (Dinesh D'Souza, The End of Racism: Principles for a Multiracial Society *[New York: Free Press, 1995], 3)*

Against this national backdrop, racist white professors are taken for granted in white academia.

This is not to suggest that our students have a natural or learned distrust of white teachers. Far from it. In our world where race matters and yet does not matter, students choose white professors as academic advisors, as directors of independent research projects, as mentors, and as friends. Therefore, when they say that a white professor is "racist" (racist here defined as one who believes blackness is synonymous with genetic inferiority and who behaves in a way to prove that it is), they are not making a blanket judgment of all white professors. Rather, they are speaking about individual professors whose racism is so obvious white peers offer them unsolicited sympathy, and, in some cases, other professors do so as well. The students get through the experience because they learned from our people getting-through/coping/overcoming techniques; and because, fortunately, those racist professors are in the minority.

If a racist is someone who has the power to translate his or her rejection of black people in a way that impacts on our reality, can a black professor with power in the academy be a racist? This was a question few in my generation had reason to ask, for only recently has white academia appointed minority faculty, which might explain, I suppose, why "diversity" is used in reference to those institutions and not to black colleges where it has been the rule rather than the exception. Hence the relevance of the question to today's black students studying away from home.

Sadly, the answer is yes. Black professors, too, have eyes that miss hands, ears that strain in order to embarrass, voices pitched in disdain, and an energy that says "you are not wanted" because you are black. They have been known to shut out, lock out, "Wite-Out," and call out black students on the basis of race, not on the basis of unsatisfactory performance. Rejection of or discomfort in the presence of those like us is one of the most damaging results of marginalization. Blacks suffer from it, as do women, Latinas, gays and lesbians, and other groups designated as "other" in mainstream American culture.

When the rejecting professor is black, however, we must be careful that we are not subjecting her or him unfairly to criteria of loyalty created by our need for special treatment. After all, black professors are not supposed to be therapists and counselors. They are scholars with all the rights and privileges that pertain to them, including the right not to be burdened with the problems of students adjusting to a new and different environment. We owe them that respect. Moreover, expecting them to identify and bond with black students is tantamount to assuming (as most white institutions assume) that they are there primarily for us; or, if not there for us, there to represent us; and if they are, then they are clearly marginalized. Resisting racism requires that we support their right to be professors, bona fide and highly credentialed, who happen to be black.

The bad news is that there are racist professors who "happen to be black"; the good news is that there are few of them. Supportive black faculty far outnumber those with closed eyes and straining ears. Along with white colleagues they teach the trees to speak our students' names, and with their own hands they open doors that want to remain only slightly ajar. They do not condescend or indulge, pamper or pity. They demand of students, as we do, the best in performance, and, like us, they make themselves available for conferences and mentoring. They are responsible for the students' first scholarly presentation at a professional meeting, their first publication in a scholarly journal, and solid contacts for the publication of their dissertations. They are in the majority. But, unfortunately, even one of us who is rejecting has the crushing weight of a throng of many when we reject in the world away from home.

This is equally true of women professors, if not more so, given our students' feminist orientation to their studies and to their naming of self. The road to white academia takes them to a feminist Mecca, for, with few exceptions, nationally known feminist scholars teach graduate students at white universities rather than undergraduates at HBCUs. Although we are optimal places for the nexus of race, gender, and class, luminaries work away from home. And studying with them is a powerful magnet attracting our students to white academia. Unfortunately, many swallow a large pill of disappointment not because of how they are treated, but rather because of the way feminist professors treat one another. The behavior is antithetical to female bonding. With disillusionment dripping in their voices, several students report division, conflict, and infighting among feminists that moves away from the arena of scholarship and toward the very personal. If racism conditions some of us to hate other blacks, it follows that misogyny conditions some women to hate other women. If in our discussion of the power of female bonding we do not underscore how far we have to go to realize it, we mislead, and therefore we impede the work of tearing down walls between us. White academia is a high-voltage, publish-or-perish environment where tenure politics produces bristling conflict rather than creative sharing; and given women scholars' struggles to dismantle centuries of white male privilege in the academy, conflicts among women scholars are to be expected. The students know this, but they are nonetheless disillusioned, and for good reason: they rarely witnessed this kind of infighting at HBCUs.

Let me quickly say that I am not claiming perfection for any historically black college. In an imperfect world, we can find perfection nowhere, only different degrees and varieties of human flaws. In our world, too, amoebae multiply in places where the water is stagnant. Class biases, color problems, sexism, homophobia, fear of differences, resistance to change—these, too, are present at HBCUs. Like professors at white schools, we are both beautiful and ugly, broad-minded and narrow, large and petty, humble and arrogant, other-directed and self-serving. We, too, fall from the grace of female bonding. We are like feminists in white academia, and yet unlike them because we work in a world so very different from theirs, a world that serves the needs of students and celebrates the art of teaching. A mission that makes students the center also protects them from being wounded in conflicts among faculty. I believe this is so at any institution that, regardless of race, amplifies the voice of those we teach rather than our own, the result of which, I believe, is a very different approach to tenure, to promotion, and to influence. Mission, then, rather than immunity to human frailties makes our conflicts sparkles that flash quickly without creating burns on our students. They might continue to burn in our memory, but they quickly extinguish themselves in the places where we serve.

After twenty-plus years at historically black colleges, I now awake with the fear that HBCUs are beginning to play with heavy explosives, so strong the wind of white validation has become. I refer here to the impact of white validation on tenure guidelines that would exact a healthy number of publications, and then only in validated journals, from a faculty committed to teaching; or on faculty searches that would give primary consideration to a record of publishing rather than a love for teaching. If we should ever adopt a white patriarchal paradigm for assessing the contributions of faculty to the education of our students, we would disconnect from our essential selves. Then our skirmishes would become battles; then we would lose even as we gain; then the students would be caught in the crossfire.

The fact is that we do not need to go that route, for we have never been simply consumers of scholarship. We have always been producers—in the traditional definition of publishing and the nontraditional definition of designing creative and cutting-edge courses. Indeed, in regard to the former, much of the touted scholarship on African-American literature that comes out of the academy leans on a foundation of scholarship first published in *The Journal of the College Language Association*, a journal housed at a black college and created when publications of the Modern Language Association did not recognize the quality of our pen. And much of the touted scholarship on African-American history and sociology first found print in *The Journal of Negro History*, *Phylon*, and other journals we "own." When the truth be told, professors at HBCUs have planted, tilled, and sowed as scholars in a number of fields. We have always been producers—lacking validation and visibility, but producers nevertheless.

I submit that racism determines the arenas in which we can show our pen, our computations, our brushes and clay, our Bunsen burners, our lasers, for the process of getting published is subjective and political, to say the least, requiring the approval of referees who constitute a small privileged group within the world of scholarship; and rarely are those referees affiliated with HBCUs. Their eyes are like the eyes of this nation. They see a black school on the letterhead, they think stereotypes, they prejudge, and they stamp "No." They see white, they prejudge, and they stamp "Yes." Both race and class operate in the process: of two manuscripts equal in quality, one from, say, Cornell will likely receive higher points than one from Ithaca College, one from Chapel Hill higher points than one from Appalachia State, one from Stanford higher points than one from San Francisco State; and a manuscript from a black school is likely to receive the lowest points of all. Regardless of the institution, if the scholar is black *and* a woman, the approving stamp is suspended in the air, waiting for someone with clout to say "Yes."

Professors at historically black institutions know what we are up against, but we do not injure ourselves when we clear publishing hurdles or weep when we cannot. That we clear them frequently, given our teaching responsibilities, makes us all the more remarkable. At Spelman, the bulletin board that announces prestigious fellowships for our students also announces autograph parties for our faculty, and departmental memoranda spread the good news about our essays in reputable journals. We are like our students in that our choice of a historically black college was an informed choice and a choice that guaranteed joys which were our desires. We know the myths about who we are, and we challenge them, and but for the knob that racism turns when it wants the volume up or down, the myths would be without sound. And the joy of this challenge is second only to the joy we experience when our students take corollary myths and hurl them into the winds. Together we are in celebration, and at any given time during the semester when we sit in the student center dialoguing with one another, we wear the same face of pleasure, satisfaction, and achievement.

By the time winter blankets the campuses with more whiteness than they ever saw at home and cold eastern winds make heavy coats shipped from home feel like drapings of gauze, the students have answered the questions, evaluated the professors, propped buildings open, worn a path from their dorms to the library, burned the midnight oil, made friends, earned respect, and pretty much mastered the game of surviving psychologically and thriving academically in this very different world. They have run the race and, with students who earned undergraduate degrees at historically white institutions, they are at the finishing gate. They can tell the trees that which we have known for over a century: to believe that students from historically black colleges are, by definition, mediocre is like believing in the prediction of rain for a day that ran its course with the sun remaining at high noon.

They have made peace with their new world, but some remain in conflict with approaches to teaching literature that, they say, distance them from the artists' visions. As one student put it, Langston Hughes's words are applicable to experiences they have had in some of their classes: "They've taken our blues and gone." The thief is consumptive theory. This is not, however, a racial problem—and students do not report it as such. Perhaps it was engendered by the discipline's need for validation in a science-obsessed nation or by tenure politics or by something inexplicable that has affected the soul of the discipline.

How unimaginable and unthinkable it is to teach a black woman's novel without teaching a black woman's experience. But it can happen! If you teach theory, theory, and more theory. Actually the problem is not theory, without which we would be crippled as a discipline, but rather the amount of it, the way it deifies the critic, the way it makes the circle of the privileged smaller, the way it validates a white male reading of black women's literature, the way it brings tenure politics into the classroom. In a world of theory-saturation, theory-dependence, and theory-consumption, you can teach *Beloved* without hearing Baby Suggs's words that the problem in the world is white folks, and, above the deadly drone of the critic who sees through a white male lens, you might never hear Suggs say, "Love yourself. . . . Love your neck. . . . Love your dark, dark liver." Hugged too closely and used in the wrong way and for the wrong reason, theory can chafe the soul and sabotage the goal of studying literature, which, I believe, is still to enlighten us about the human experience, the human condition, and to engage us thus enlightened in the universal/eternal discussion on truth and justice.

English faculty in institutions all across the nation, regardless of race, have the same concern the students have, but we voice it only in private conversations among ourselves. To speak out is to risk being called unknowing or anti-intellectual. For my students, I take that risk.

Several years ago, I wrote an entry in my journal entitled

"Requiem for a Love." The love was black women's literature which was sometimes made unrecognizable in criticism that killed another love—language. It is sometimes so cold this language, sometimes unfathomable, deliberately unfathomable; a mausoleum of syllables that have no breath, no soul; a language that obfuscates that which is supposed to inform, enlighten, humanize, transform, and transport to realms of feeling and being mere words cannot describe. I wrote that in the plethora of ize-words (problematize, historicize, sexualize, racialize, valorize, scientize) I could find little of the beauty and simplicity that moved me as a teenager and later motivated me to become a teacher of literature, sending me joyous to critical essays on works I loved—then (before black studies and women's studies) novels by black men like Wright and Ellison and by white men like Lawrence and Joyce. The beauty of a critical essay on *Sons and Lovers* took me orbiting into my dream of being a college professor who transmitted to students this, my love.

This was the same dream of a young white woman in her mid-thirties I met several years ago at a book fair in Atlanta. When I congratulated her on the success of her two books, she read from the diary of her graduate school memories a requiem similar to mine. Consumptive theory, she said, that deprived her of intimacy with writers caused her to drop her English major and exit with a doctorate in clinical psychology. She gave up on the discipline. Our students are staying the course. To complete it, they must make use of survival motions that are theirs by virtue of who they are and what they must do. Those of us who have earned terminal degrees, regardless of the institution or our race, know all too well that attempting to change the ordering principles of our programs is suicidal. Life beyond graduate school is our students' goal. Therefore, they master the theory, but in the quiet of their rooms, they read Baby Suggs's sermon in the clearing.

Finally, and on time, they reach that stage in a graduate student's life that is both heaven and hell—heaven because writing the dissertation means they are probably on their way out, but hell because dissertation politics can be to graduate students what tenure politics is to professors. Hell. During their three or four years of study, students might witness the effects of the tenure process: near nervous breakdowns, changes in personality, changes in ideology, termination of old friendships, creation of new friendships, weight gain or weight loss, and explosions of hidden mines in the field, which one student called "backstabbing." As spectators (and in some cases as participants caught in the crossfire of tenure politics), wise graduate students learn to be politically astute in the composition of their committees, for how the committee works is as vital to the completion of the dissertation as how well they think, research, and write. They are immersed, then, in politics, politics, politics.

This professor would be supportive, but knows nothing about the subject. That one knows the subject but two years ago left the country and the student whose dissertation was near completion. Lightning can strike twice! This one would insist on including a writer not major to the vision of the dissertation. That one voted no to a colleague's tenure request, citing as reason she wasn't "postmodern enough." Lightning can strike twice. This one reads with her eye on signs of racial essentialist thinking. That one with her eye on nothing other than her own research. This one worships Derrida. That one talks nothing except Spivak. This one is a voice in the neoconservative movement. That one is at odds with the movement. This one accepts the scholarship of black feminist critics. That one does not. Marxist, liberal, modernist, postmodernist . . . Politics. Politics. Politics.

"What else is new?" they ask us, demonstrating an attitude that says they can see their exit. "We find politics in all experiences involving human beings."

"How right you are about that!" we say. "Politics in the church, politics in families, politics in organizations committed to changing politics. And so, how did you choose?"

They don't mix oil and water, but neither do they cast their ideas out for anybody's catch to be placed face down in anybody's current. They choose politically, but with integrity; and that they can so choose speaks to the good in white academia and to the good people, black and white, male and female, in white academia. They secure signatures from professors who are humanists, passionate about truth and research and supportive of students who are for them, as for us, the reason they remain in the profession, awaking each day renewed by its call.

And then comes the conversation we never discussed in their leave-taking because my generation was never privy to it in our graduate school experiences. You see, white academia *has* changed. A short time ago (like three decades short), a black academician could be the most brilliant of scholars, the most talented with words, numbers, and equations, a scholar's scholar; but only home believed in such professors and only home took them in. The exigencies of black life then and the invisibility of black students at white schools made home more than the place Robert Frost describes as when you go there, they have to take you in. Home was where black academicians wanted to go, where they were needed, where they would continue to grow in their various disciplines, and where they were sent with white academia's blessings.

"What are your plans?" professors ask today's young black intellectuals, impressed, as we knew they would be, with our students' talents.

"Let me give you some good advice," the professors say. "Don't teach at a black school. It would be a loss. A terrible loss of your talents."

Only the exceptional among our students "merit" this advice. Those who are average are expected to rush home for the same reason that we remain at home: to be big fish in a small pond. This was the assessment a nationally known black scholar at an Ivy League institution made of black college faculty. According to him, we love the sound of our splash in the pond and since the water level is low, the only stroke we need to learn is the elementary freestyle.

To go home again or not: that is the dilemma of today's young black intellectuals.

Before this conversation, some had already decided not to go home again, having been seduced upon entering this world by the buildings, the acres, the money, and the power, and by the certitude of access to research, to publications, to validation, to all the getting things. Like the young man in Ellison's *Invisible Man*, some began immediately to stand before an imaginary mirror, tilting their heads at the most becoming angle and practicing how to move their hands to the rhythm of applause. Early on, home became the place where when you go there, they take you in with love and ask you to serve with love, but, offering less than you can get away from home, it is where you do not want to go. For some, it becomes where you do not remember ever having been. Forgetting is always easier than remembering, especially if what we forget the nation rejects.

We see these students at MLA meetings en route to interviews for jobs away from home. They smile, wave hello, and never stop to talk. We have some ownership in what we are experiencing because we taught them that MLA, which once denied us membership, is the sine qua non of professional organizations. We failed to teach them the history of CLA, which was founded by us to serve our needs and which, as long as MLA kept its doors open, was a strong professional organization for professors at black institutions, regardless of race. Today CLA struggles to survive because annually—at the worst of times for women and for men as well, Christmas holidays designed for families regardless of religious convictions—we board planes in the cold winters to be counted among those validated. Perhaps we taught our students how to forget.

Ironically, the students afflicted with amnesia are the ones we lauded the most, put on the highest pedestal; gems we, with our own hands, polished to the brightest shine. In our letters of recommendation we said they could walk on water, sure that they could, for we had seen them emerge with dry feet having been fathoms deep in academic rigor. One brief walk around the walls of ivy, and they become vaunted with vanity and fearful of losing the validation they have earned. The fear produces only astigmatism at first, then, progressing, becomes an illness, the symptoms of which are very noticeable. The corners of the mouth twist at the mention of home and the lips stretch into a broad smile at the mention of any place but home. Professors away from home are gods dispensing blessings inside the temple; professors at home are flawed mortals standing outside and begging to enter. If by chance they return home for founders' day or alumni celebrations, they do so to advertise where they are, not where they came from. They dress themselves from head to toe in away-from-home paraphernalia and bumper their cars with their new, and now permanent, address. If by chance they remain on campus long enough for closing ceremonies, they substitute alma mater lyrics that made them the center of our world with words that do not yet recognize their existence. They forget but, worse, they denigrate. These students should not return, and do not.

If, by chance, they return some years down the road—and often many do—no one will raise questions about where they have been, because what will matter more than the when of their coming is what they bring with them: reclaimed memories and a dedication to the mission of the institution.

Some of them do not come home again for very different

reasons, and here I refer to students who turn a deaf ear to racist nonsense that seeks to marginalize us in higher education. They are the students who remember home and attribute to home their many achievements. For them, home "made all the difference," and at the slightest hint of denigration of home, they will enrobe themselves as warriors. Home is that special place in their hearts, that place where they name themselves, but that place to which they cannot return. Will they be able to write at home? Yes, but only after they have fulfilled their obligations to students. Will they be published at home? Yes, but with difficulty. Will their publications receive the attention they deserve? Perhaps yes and perhaps no. It depends on so very much over which home has no control. The fact is, we can offer them no guarantee that they will realize their goal of being a writer while working at home, and, since that is their passion, we understand why they will not take the risk. Not everyone is a risk-taker. Moreover, not everyone can teach and produce scholarship. Wearing two hats, and wearing them well, is for some people like a trick needing puffs of smoke and magic wands. Students who want more than anything to write will not come home again and perhaps should not. We congratulate them on their appointments away from home, knowing that in their classes, in their departmental meetings, and in all of their professional comings and goings, they will take home with them.

Some of them should not come home because we must be *everywhere* in academia—as tenured professors, as chairs of departments, as directors of programs, as editors of journals, as scholars, as provosts, as presidents—perhaps most especially in those places that in the past denied us admission. To have the *choice* to teach away from home is an indisputable gain, but like so many other gains we achieved from the struggle in which both blacks and whites risked and gave their lives, it comes with losses we either did not anticipate or anticipated but without understanding the full measure of their impact on our reality. If race is the American dilemma, racial progress could well become the black American dilemma, for we have not discovered how to achieve racial justice and at the same time retain visibility and voice, strength and self-esteem, in the places where, prior to progress, we had both. The more impressive the progress, the more frightening the possibility of erasure. Hence my passionate belief that while some of our students should teach away from home, celebrating the hard-won *choice*, some must come home again in order to serve a new generation of young black intellectuals. If, for various reasons—absence of jobs in white academia, denial of tenure there, a genuine commitment to our mission, a desire to work at black institutions for reasons they need not explain or simply a desire to teach without regard for the race of the students or the racial history of the institution—white academicians are the principal applicants for recruitment, historically black colleges will indeed be in need of "diversity."

I could understand why professors might say "Do not teach at a black college" if they offered our students good reasons for their advice. Several come to mind: The discipline they want to teach is not offered there; their love is research rather than teaching; they are introverts and therefore ill-suited for mentoring; or they are simply not cut out to wear several hats well. I could appreciate the advice if the professors were interested in the welfare of black students at historically white institutions: "They need you as much as students at black schools need you, perhaps more." And I could Amen the advice if the professors were steering our students away from the ranks of the ABDs (All But the Dissertation): "I understand your desire to return and I know you will do good work there, but you should finish your dissertation first and get it published." Unfortunately, when students hear the advice, they hear only an impugning of the academic integrity of historically black institutions: "Do not return because inferiority is there." Sadly, most of the professors who offer this acid advice are African-American. One brief second ago, many of them would have been forced to teach where they now advise our students not to go.

Where did it come from, this need to denigrate black institutions? Whom does it serve? And how? As one colleague said after MLA, "Contention between professors at historically black colleges and historically white ones is pervasive, even palpable." Why is opositionality the nature of our relationship? I know of no evidence that suggests it is the nature of the relationship between whites who teach at different historically white institutions.

I acknowledge that what I call "home" is not home for many of today's black academicians in white academia, for like many of us who choose home, working there as presidents, deans, and faculty, they did not attend a historically black undergraduate college and they have never lived in a predominantly black environment. But I submit that regardless of where we earned our degrees and where we have lived, or live, we must be aware as African-Americans of the importance, the history, and the impressive track record of historically black institutions and, as well, of our need and the nation's need for the continued existence and strengthening of those institutions, individually and collectively. In my opinion, there can be no justification for any African-American scholar to use her or his words and time, influence and clout, to undermine black schools. I ask again, for what reason and to serve whom?

If we advocate for dialog between blacks and whites, women and men, people of color and those not of color, gays and heterosexuals, shouldn't we also advocate for dialog between two important and very different groups in higher education: black academicians at black colleges and black academicians at white colleges? We are different, working in different worlds, and seeing, in some instances, with different eyes. I say we must talk because, whether we accept it or not, we are the role models for today's black students and all of them, regardless of the originating institution, are needed. Our arrangement as strangers, and especially as antagonists, serves them ill. I say we must talk because I believe there is a direct correlation between changes that will take place for the masses of our people and our ability to talk to each other, just as there is a direct correlation between politics in the nation and politics in the academy. I say we must talk because our coming together could make us a formidable voice for change in this nation, not just for our people, but for all people.

In the silence that divides us, there is the loud "Yes!" of young black intellectuals who intend to fix what is broken in the academy and to remain in communication with one another. I hear this intention in conversations with students who are taking home with them to white institutions and with those who are choosing to come home again. Each will appreciate, value, and support in whatever way she or he can the work the other is doing.

Why will some of them choose home? They will tell you that they never left home with the intention of not returning. They never had a dilemma. They are attracted to the magical way we balance sacrifice and reward. They have no illusions about home and therefore they know they will give up much, but they are certain they will get more in return. And although they cannot quantify what they will receive, they know it has inestimable value for our people, for the nation, and no less for themselves. They return home because home feels good to them spiritually, politically, and academically. Home is in their viscera, in their memory, in their vision of intellectual stretching for women and men like themselves— determined to achieve and anxious to make a difference. At home they pass on to future generations our people's legacy of achievement and struggle. They are psychologists ensuring the health of their students, for they believe that the health of any people is measured by the commitment some among them make to institutions immersed in their history and their culture. They are scholars—passionate about their work—who believe that knowledge is not its own excuse for being; knowledge has meaning when it has relevance to humanity and power when it effects change. They are celebrants in a ritual that recognizes our many and distinctive successes and repairwomen who work to fix broken places. Primarily, they are teacher-artists who cannot breathe without creating their art, and for them, historically black colleges are the canvases on which the colors of their paints are never muted and their creative designs are never obscured. That they come home again ensures the survival, the strengthening, and the impressive uniqueness of home. If by some miracle the so-called millennium arrives, they know that home will not vanish in the new air. It will continue to exist, offering to other students who choose home the gifts we have given black students for over a century.

6

When Race Is Memory
and Blackness Is Choice

I was second in line at a K-Mart located on Bankhead Avenue, a two-lane busy thoroughfare that made national and international news almost a decade ago as the community in which four victims of the Atlanta child murders lived and that today often makes local news when the subject is drug violence. Bankhead is cluttered with fast-food chains, automobile junkyards, dress shops, bars, and liquor stores. I have driven down it so many times I know the exact location of R & M Fashions, Keyta's Kleaners, Payless Shoes, and the Shell Service Station where, for the past five months, a yellow poster propped in the window has advertised a weekly event which, in promoting pagers, a nicer word for beepers, supports drug trafficking in the community: "Phat Friday's. Talent Competition. $200.00 Cash Prize. Free *Pager*. Sponsored by the Citywide Pager Association" (italics mine). Bankhead is a street I reach in a five-minute's drive from my house.

I had shopped at the K-Mart many times for items like paper towels, safety pins, and washing detergent, but this time I had gone specifically to catch bargains in a Happy New Year sale: everything that had been stocked in 1995 was fifty percent off. Either the bargains did not exist or they were hidden in the clutter piled high in baskets that blocked aisles. It would have been a wasted trip had I not been invited to participate in playful bantering, one of the cultural rhythms that took me to this store located on such a dangerous street and to other places located on safer streets where black people gather.

"Is this check gonna bounce?" the cashier asked a man in his fifties as he wrote a check without the benefit of stands raised waist high at stores in other neighborhoods. The counter was his desk.

"As high as the Harlem Globetrotters," the man said.

They laughed. I laughed. The woman behind me laughed. Everyone in line laughed.

The cashier involved me in the game. "Do you know this man?" she asked. No one can be only a spectator in black bantering. "If you don't, you're one lucky woman."

The line laughed.

"You always have it in for me when I come in here," the man said, picking up the thin plastic bag that advertised his purchases, among them items I no longer buy but that were once on shopping lists I took to the store in my old neighborhood: a jar of Palmolive hair oil, a box of Ex-Lax, a package of hairpins, and a jar of Vaseline.

"Well, why do you always come through my line?" she asked, reaching for the items I am purchasing. "Why don't you go to Marie?"

The woman at the cash register to our right quickly said, "I know you *didn't* try to send him over to me."

The line laughed again. The man laughed loudest of all.

He lingered near the register as the cashier began ringing up my purchases—Bounty towels, plant food, and a squeaky toy for my frisky puppy.

"Price check," she called, tapping a lightly ringing bell. I should have known that without a cellophane package, the squeaky toy could not have a price.

"That's okay," I quickly said, not wanting to inconvenience people behind me. "I really don't need it." The line breathed a sigh of relief.

"Now why can't you be nice like this woman?" the cashier said to the man who was lingering still.

"There you go again picking on me," he said through laughter. "You are one cranky woman."

"And you are one pitiful man," she responded.

Black bantering often ends with an announcement that it has been bantering all along. As in, "I was just kidding" or "This keeps our blood pressure down" or "We like to mess with each other."

That's what the cashier said: "Don't mind us. We always mess with each other. He's my neighbor."

He bantered again: "But I live on the pretty side of the street."

"And, girl, can he sing?" She had packaged my purchases.

"Are you gonna do a solo this Sunday?" she asked the man while pulling new purchases toward her. Unlike those at other stores, this counter does not move items to the reaching hand.

I heard them talking church—"You know we got a guest preacher this Sunday," the man said—as I left the store, walking past a deli where pork hot dogs were sold and stale popcorn looked more yellow than white in a bin that needed cleaning.

Outside women, many with children, were reaching for grocery carts with rusty wheels and pushing them through the doors of a store that stands to the right of K-Mart, a store I entered but will not enter again. A distinct odor of rancid meat, primarily pork, identifies it as one of the many groceries located in black inner-city communities. Everything about the store and in the store says that throwaways are being sold to people who do not matter. The lettuce is brown, the cabbage is limp, and the fruit is so overripe it is bruised by the mere touch of your fingers. As you move up and down aisles that need sweeping, you feel eyes watching you, stalking you.

I wanted to stop the women from entering the store and direct them to stores with bright lights, clean floors, wide aisles, fresh produce, and fish fresh from the water. Stores that sell respect with a smile. But those stores are not located in this world. They were not built to serve people who are paying with food stamps or with the money left over after they pay ten percent to have their small checks cashed at centers that jut out from every corner in these neighborhoods. Centers that take utility payments for a fee. Centers that sell beepers. "Cheap," the signs read. "No credit check. No down payment."

The people who sell the beepers are like those who sell other items in this community. They are invaders and card-carrying exploiters who wear a different face. The liquor

stores, many in number, are run by people who come from
the other side of the ocean where even the horizon seems to
be a vast stretch of a sandy desert. The nail places, also many
in number, are operated by people whose alphabet does not
appear on the dollar bills that pay for acrylic nails covered
with balloons or roses. The wig shops, which are next door to
nail shops, are run by women who have no need for wigs. The
service stations (for quik-shopping) are operated by men
whose hair is slightly wooly, but whose skin color and features
save them from identification with the people who buy the
overpriced beer, soda pop, and sanitary napkins.

Sometimes, but less often than in the past, the store own-
ers who exploit them speak their language, wear their features, and check black or African-American on their driver's
license. In a similar neighborhood in North Carolina, the
man who broke my '83 Nissan in order to render it beyond
the repair he had promised—"Your engine is just plumb
gone"—was very dark skinned, a Baptist church Christian,
and a raconteur who enchanted me with tales that began,
"Sweet Pea, you won't believe this but back when I was living
in the country . . ." The merchant a block away from my
house who sells stale bread for two dollars was born in Nigeria, grew up in Nigeria, and left Nigeria in order to come to
a neighborhood like this one to exploit people who look
like him and who call the place from which he came their
"Motherland." The black woman in corn rows at a variety
store who sells a slim roll of cellophane tape for two dollars
to children purchasing supplies for school projects gives no
currency to racial/cultural sisterhood. In a nation where

profit matters more than people, black merchants, too, exploit us—and us rather than whites only because they are not cleared for visibility in those neighborhoods. They exploit us and if we are poor, they denigrate us. That is what the people in the Bankhead community experience: exploitation and denigration.

I am close to this community, a block away, but I live in a world of houses and well-kept lawns where middle-class and lower-middle-class blacks can come together in community meetings for the latest contact or number that will give us immediate responses to our requests for service. They live in a world of apartment complexes where there are units needing repair or units boarded up and concrete where once there was earth. They live in the inner city where they have neither the contact nor the number.

After the trauma of an attempted rape, I thought about running far away from the city, running and forgetting, running and screaming, running and never looking back. Running to the assumed safety and security of suburbia. But a strange something that runs from the top of my head to the soles of my feet, moving unobstructed through my heart, checked me in flight. "Where would you like to look?" the realtor asked. "Near my people" was my answer.

My people are doctors, dentists, attorneys, academicians, morticians, bankers, realtors; shoe repairmen, florists, mechanics, locksmiths, beauticians; artists, poets, and dancers; professionals, semi-professionals, craftsmen, artisans, skilled and unskilled workers who are doing well and living well enough to have comfort and security, medical insurance and retirement, dreams in the making and dreams already realized.

I see them when I go to the neighborhood black bank where black women wearing perms or braids orchestrate the moving of lines that are too long to windows that are too few in number. On emotionally rainy days, I think about taking my money to branches of white-owned banks located in white neighborhoods where the windows are many and the lines move fast, but that strange something turns my attention from the inconvenience I experience to the connection I have with the people in line. Each time I am there, something lifts me in a way I cannot explain. Last week, it was the baritone voice of a man behind me speaking loudly and lovingly to an elderly man he called "Dad" and then apologizing to me for the volume: "He doesn't hear well anymore." The week before it was a good-to-see-you hug from a woman with whom I had worked in the PTA when my children were in high school ten years ago.

I see my people in the shoe repair shop where a pencil-thin man with a pencil-thin moustache works magic resoling old shoes; in the professional building where my children years ago rode the elevators to the sixth floor to the orthodontist who tightened their braces; in the waiting room of the Morehouse Medical School Associates where patients, most of them women with children or elderly parents, wait to see black doctors, women and men, who know their family history without reading the charts; in the herbal shop where a man wearing locks and a woman wearing braids offer cures the doctors have not yet discovered; and in the Atlanta Uni-

versity Center where faculty, staff, and students walk self-
affirmed and somewhat arrogant in a world they know to be
their own. These are my people; they are doing well; and
from them I get my name.

But my people are also the women, men, and children who
are not doing well. Who push rusty-wheeled carts into grocery stores where they buy inferior goods at high prices with
food stamps we are now saying they do not deserve. Who
have no orthodontist appointments for their children or
medical appointments for themselves. Who have no bank accounts. Who have no jobs. They are "the masses" in this nation who live in inner-city communities bounded by streets
like Bankhead.

They are the people Newt Gingrich and others of contract
mentality would have us believe are responsible for socioeconomic ills that plague this nation. They could change the parameters of their lives, contract thinking tells us, if they but
chose to do so. Such thinking is tantamount to believing that
the poor among my people can just say "no," using E-mail
perhaps, to the big guys overseas and those on these shores,
and drugs will no longer be distributed in their neighborhoods because they will have learned to value their children
more than their Swiss bank accounts; that they could, if they
but cared, establish a humane health care delivery system,
build decent housing, and create a public school system committed to education rather than to the "savage inequality"
Jonathan Kozol documents as one of the most egregious sins
in this nation; that they have the know-how to reduce our national debt without cutting programs that serve people, including themselves; indeed, that they have the power to de-

liver unto all Americans, themselves not excluded, the inalienable rights of "life, liberty and the pursuit of happiness." They are the people our nation brutalizes with impunity. That they are makes my identification with them, the naming of myself with their names, so very necessary and urgent. In a sense, they are more "my people" than those among my people who have not yet been brutalized. Politics aside, however, I know they are my people because in their features I see my own face and in the way they walk, laugh, and gesticulate with their hands I feel rhythms that are as natural to me as breathing and perhaps as needed as air.

Choosing them as my people does not serve any of their needs, for, to be honest, though I live only two blocks away from Bankhead, I have not screamed enough about what is happening in that world. When I turn on the evening news and hear that four people were killed in a drug-related shootout on Bankhead Highway, not far from where the K-Mart is located and where the woman in corn rows slams down my change, or three people were burned to death in a house four blocks away and four doors down from where my friend Geraldine lives, the house to which I go for bonding and political dialog—burned to death when their kerosene stove tipped over—I weep, I feel a weighty sadness, I breathe anger deep into my lungs, but I fall asleep in a house with a security system and central heat that comes on without a sound. I scream before I fall asleep, but when I awake the next morning, I do nothing to challenge the devastation that ravages their world. I rationalize that without a movement there is nothing I can do.

If choosing to remain in a predominantly black community not far from the world of violence does not serve my people—makes me rather sanctimonious perhaps—why then do I choose? One answer to this question is "Guilt." I experience it frequently, though my friend Helen corrects me and says it is not guilt, but concern. She is correct. It is concern, but that I do not express the concern in action converts it to guilt. I cannot see poor African-Americans without feeling that something I did or did not do accounts in part for their difficulties. I do not buy brand names, do not drive a fancy car, and my house is one of the most modest on my street. I do not overspend or conspicuously spend. And yet knowing that, compared to them, I have so much, perhaps more than I need or deserve, I feel guilty.

"I don't feel guilty," a woman said during a dialog following a reading from *Pushed Back to Strength* in Martinez, California. She screamed at me. "And I don't intend to be made to feel guilty." She had worked hard for everything she possessed and, what's more, she had her own problems in white America. As Ellie Cose in *The Rage of a Privileged Class* and Joe Feagin and Melvin Sikes in *Living with Racism: The Black Middle-Class Experience* document, middle-class blacks have reason to be in a state of rage. I believe our rage spins in a way that it does not spin for poor blacks. They do not expect justice and fair play. We do. We went the extra miles to guarantee that both would be ours, but both often elude us. Hence a rage that promises not delivered exacerbates; a rage that can explode in the least expected of places and at the least expecting of individuals.

Unbridled rage was what I felt when my nephew, a geologist trained at Northwestern, was accosted by white police while he was on his way home from the library—the *library!* First there was the sound of screeching tires and then the order, "Halt!" They rushed toward him and slammed him face down on the pavement in a cold Virginia winter, handcuffed his hands behind his back and held a gun against his head. He begged them to check his ID which confirmed that he was an environmental scientist working for the government, but they did not listen. Face down, he heard the call for backup, minutes later the screeching tires, and within seconds the words that saved him: "This is not the suspect." The black man who had robbed a white woman was wearing a green jacket and a baseball cap. My nephew, bareheaded, was wearing an overcoat.

I know that we as middle-class blacks are victimized by racism in this nation, but when I think about how much poor African-Americans are denied and how brutally they are violated, I scream more for them than I do for us. This scream does not mean, however, that I agree with the author of an article published several years ago in *The Atlantic Monthly* which placed on the shoulders of the black middle class the responsibility for saving the poor among our people. This responsibility belongs to *all* of us, but less to the few blacks living in the world of the glass ceiling than to those who put the ceiling in place and whose loud voice of power and dominance, hitting high racist octaves, can shatter it, sending the broken pieces into our veins. Like other middle-class blacks, I, too, am tired of white people trying to make me feel guilty, but white people are not the people I hear when guilt speaks to me. It is, rather, the voice of women and men from my old neighborhood reminding me never to forget from whence and whom I came. They don't say, "Feel guilty." They say only, "Remember."

To ensure that I do not forget is the reason I choose to remain in a black community. I am, in essence, serving my own emotional needs rather than the needs of my people. It is my way of always being where I can see them coming and going and to be reminded, therefore, of who I am and whose I am. It is my way of knowing that buffeted though they are by fierce winds, like my people at other times and in other places, they have created a world the winds do not penetrate—a world enriched by rituals, by affectionate bantering, by analyses in their/our own language of what is wrong with this country, by the way they name themselves and claim themselves, by an awareness of being alive and together in a way that makes them and their own the center of their world, and by the color of their dreams for their children. It is my way of guaranteeing that I will never make the mistake of seeing them through rejecting eyes—a mistake so easily made in a nation as polarized by class as it is by race. When we do not see the poor among our people coming and going in their humanity—we might be seeing them as "those" people rather than as "our" people—then we will judge them harshly. "Those people" have nails that show the residue of work and, if they are young, nails that display the extent to which they have been seduced by salons selling balloons on acrylic at a handsome price. We have well-manicured nails sans balloons. "Those people" rub their legs with Vaseline.

We stroke our legs with Nivea and other expensive lotions. "Those people" wear pink rollers (in grocery stores at that!). We wear fine coiffures created in well-lighted salons. "Those people" carry the aroma of garlic, a miracle cure for the poor. We waft with the fragrance of Calyx, Obsession or Anaïs Anaïs. But we are "those people" in the new clothes that luck—or, as the old folks say, "the grace of God"—gave us.

What I am seeking, then, when I choose to live in a black community where I can see my people is the gift of memory, a gift so precious that without it no person is whole or, for that matter, happy. Anyone without a connection to her race, or her people, experiences, I believe, a dryness in the throat that makes singing of self impossible.

Race. I know I should not use that word for, as the experts tell us, it does not exist. Race? It has no basis in science. When I read essays that elucidate this truth, I turn to Langston Hughes for words that will express simply how I feel. People in Harlem, he wrote, had not heard that the "Negro was in vogue," and if they had, they would testify that it didn't change their reality one bit. Black people in inner cities are not aware of the scholarship that proves race cannot be defined and does not exist, but if they were, I believe they would doubt that the scholarship has any bearing on their lives and find it strange that, in these troubled times, anyone would believe that what has been the cause of their exploitation— named as cause by pundits and scholars, spiritual leaders and political activists—no longer exists. If I am guilty here of using the no-longer-acceptable language of victimology, blame it on my eyes, for they have seen people who are, in fact, victims of economic brutality because of their race. At a time when, as Derrick Bell tells us, the deep dye of racism has revealed itself to be a permanent stain in the American fabric, for me, the intellectual dialog—Is race is or is race ain't?—has a hollow ring. Like chamber music, it is sometimes played in a small room to a select and self-selected audience.

I guess that is my way of expressing concern that the conservatism we see in national politics is taking up residence in the academy, even in the wing where some black intellectuals are housed. When I become disillusioned with this group, albeit a minority among black intellectuals, or confused by the spin they put on dialog on race and racial essentialism, I find myself wishing that W. E .B. Du Bois were still among us. In all of his scholarship, he was clear that his focus was on Negroes, Negro Americans, the folk, the people, us, the "Negro race." This clarity about who he was and on whose behalf he was using his genius in part explains, I believe, why he chose to die, not in Europe, but in Africa. Moreover, his scholarship, second in brilliance to no other, always had resonance and meaning beyond the chamber, for at its center was Du Bois's insistence on change in this nation that would impact the lives of the folk. Indeed, the "talented tenth" has as its mission the delivery of this change.

Desperate for poignant and compelling words that speak for me in today's intellectual dialog on race, I cling to phrases and sentences that seem to jump from the pages of Du Bois's essays, giving me permission to take them out of the context of his brilliance and place them in the context of my need. Although race transcends scientific definition, Du Bois wrote, it is "clearly defined to the eye of the Historian and Sociologist," and, therefore, "the history of the world is the history, not of individuals, but of groups, not of nations, but of races.

> *What, then, is a race? It is a vast family of human beings, generally of common blood and language, always of common history, traditions and impulses, who are both voluntarily and involuntarily striving together for the accomplishment of certain more or less vividly conceived ideals of life. (David Leuering Lewis, ed.,* W. E. B. Du Bois: A Reader *[New York: Holt Publishers, 1995], 21)*

The people in the Bankhead community and black people in other communities in Atlanta and in other cities belong to the "vast family" I choose as my own. We have in common blood, language, history, traditions, impulses—race.

If race is problematic, blackness is even more so. It can't be defined, scholars tell us, at least not in one all-applying way. In the past, we said no to a monolithic reading of blackness. Today we say no to racial essentialism. Same thought, different semantics. Racial essentialism hurts all of us, the masses and the middle class, and in that it serves racist ends, it must be challenged.

Away from the world of academia, I worry about the timing of this debate. Of course truth is no respecter of timing. Truth *is* regardless of time, place, gender, race, religion, sexual orientation. That is what makes it *truth*. While I know that timing does not alter truth, I believe it can affect the way truth is used, and by whom. Which is why I am concerned about the truth of the racial essentialist debate. It is, without question, a brilliant dethroning of racist myths, but I worry that it can easily be misconstrued by men with evil minds who have targeted black people, especially the masses, for a dispossession that will move from obsolescence to extinction. We can say, "That is not what we meant," but men with evil minds can say: "You see, even their own people are saying they should stop with this business about race and blackness." I wonder if there is a way to clothe truth—not disguise it, but clothe it—in a protective *seal* so tight evil men cannot unwrap it and use truth for nefarious goals? But why ask such an inane question when truth, by its very nature, is available to all.

The source of my concern might be less the debate and more the new language that identifies us as a group. No longer is it politically correct to say "black people." Instead, we must say "people of color." Since erasure or a new kind of marginalization could result from this naming—especially in this era of insidious racism—I identify myself as a black woman ("of African descent" is my preference). That is how other people of color see me, people who, being very American, often choose to identify with whites rather than blacks. Hatred of people of African descent remains in the psyche of this nation. Indeed, as Andrew Hacker writes in *Two Nations*, black and white are still the defining words for lack of influence and influence. While being white does not "automatically" bring success and status, Hacker writes, "What it does ensure is that [no white person] will be regarded as *black*, a security that is worth so much that no one who has it has ever given it away."

Actually, what troubles me is that in this era of renaming, which seems at times to be un-naming, we go beyond proving that blackness has so many and varied characteristics it can't be defined to positing that it simply does not exist. In a word, we throw it away. It has no history, no culture, no rituals, no face. It is perhaps nothing more than a figure of speech. It meant so much to us, our claiming and celebration of what we called/call blackness! It removed streaks and cracks from the mirror in which for so long we had been forced to see ourselves! Please, I want to scream, please don't take it away. Not now. Not when the winds are so very cold and fierce. Please do not send us naked into white America.

Were I a scholar I would probably not be troubled by this disavowal of blackness, for I would work my way through its layers of complexity to acceptance, but I am less a scholar and more a woman of memory. Can memory explain what it is I possess, what I defend, what I will *not* give away. And as long as the racial waters in white America crash against the reality of my people with the force of hurricanes of hatred, I will hold on to my blackness with tenacity.

Memory tells me that blackness is in my essence as surely as blood is in my veins. It is an antenna I do not always know I am wearing, but which is surely there, identifying me as a woman who belongs to a group different in particularities from women who are Asian, Latina, Chicana, Native American, or Jewish. It is the music of songs I learned from I do not know where, but which I find myself singing. It is a way of seeing myself and seeing others like me through a lens that never closes.

It is an inexpressible something expressed with brilliance and compelling passion in the fiction of Toni Morrison or in the essays of James Baldwin, speaking in a voice assuredly its own; a soulful something we hear in the spirituals, the gospel, and the blues, the lining songs, which resist notation on a line through which a G clef is neatly drawn; a rhythm that makes us wave our hands a certain way when we talk, when we walk, when we laugh, and even when we cry; a color we weave into quilts we once did not value; a texture we feel when we touch truths and untruths with our own hands; rituals we observe which we do not call rituals, so natural they are and so necessary to so much of what we do; a time and place, an experience, that anchors us in a unique history we do not yet completely understand; and a way we lean into the winds, lean into them. But all of this might be but tropes, not definitions or explanations. I could say that my blackness, like my woman-ness, which is never separate from my blackness, is, to borrow from Du Bois, that something "in the marrow of [my] bones" (Herbert Aptheker, ed. *The Education of Black People: Ten Critiques, 1906–1960, by W. E .B. Du Bois* [New York: Monthly Review Press, 1973], 143).

Can anyone define blackness? Should anyone attempt to? For me, the only answer to this question is another question: Toward what end and for whom? At another time, the millennium time, perhaps we could plunge deep into our people's history and culture, memory and soul, to discover parts that add up to a recognizable whole we can call blackness and then "throw it away," or place it in a museum, because in the millennium time it would have no relevance, no meaning, no existence. But not now. Not now when the people are literally being tossed about in the fiercest of winds. Not now.

I believe that if Du Bois were alive, his prophecy for the new century might well be the prophecy he made in the nineteenth century for the one we will soon exit: the problem of the twentieth century, he wrote, will be the color line. The signs now suggest that the problem of the twenty-first century will be the color line, or race, and therefore also gender and class, for those are the three axes on which power and influence continue to turn in this nation.

Given the signs, there is only one New Year's resolution for a black woman of memory: to do more than call my people "my people" and do more than choose to live where I can see them/us coming and going in their/our humanity. I, therefore, resolve to work with other groups, regardless of their gender, religious persuasion, or sexual preference and regardless of any nonscientific racial category in which we place them, to end the violence which is pervasive in the lives of the poor among my people and the lives of the poor among other people. To borrow from Du Bois's moving tribute to black women, the women of his race he called us, "this small thing," this commitment to struggle, I owe my people for the gift of memory.

LIBRARY OF CONGRESS CATALOGING-IN-PUBLICATION DATA

Wade-Gayles, Gloria Jean.
 Rooted against the wind : personal essays / Gloria Wade-Gayles.
  p. cm.
   1. Wade-Gayles, Gloria Jean. 2. Afro-Americans—Biography.
3. Afro-American women—Biography. 4. Afro-American women—
Social conditions. 5. Afro-Americans—Intellectual life. I. Title.
E185.97.W126A3 1996
305.89'6073'092—dc20   96-12167